Beth Montgomery was born in Greece and has lived in England and Hell's Kitchen New York. She moved permanently to the UK where she pursued various careers such as Fashion Illustration and Freelance Journalism, before embarking in a long career in healthcare. Until everything changed in one night. Do you believe in luck? Beth didn't till the unbelievable happened.

This book was written in loving memory of Michael, and Lilly who are gone but not forgotten, and above all for our amazing Doctors, Nurses, and Care Assistants, our unsung heroes.

Beth Montgomery

LIFE AND DEATH

A True Account of Life
on the Front Line Told
by a Nurse

AUSTIN MACAULEY PUBLISHERS®

LONDON • CAMBRIDGE • NEW YORK • SHARJAH

A CIP catalogue record for this title is available from the British Library.

ISBN 9781398432543 (Paperback)
ISBN 9781398432550 (ePub e-book)

www.austinmacauley.com

First Published 2025
Austin Macauley Publishers Ltd®
1 Canada Square
Canary Wharf
London
E14 5AA

I would like to thank all the team at Austin Macauley who saw my potential and didn't reject my manuscript and worked tirelessly to make this happen. I'd also like to offer my gratitude and thanks to the doctors and fellow nurses who saved my life they are my heroes; without them I wouldn't be here so for that I am eternally grateful.

"An honest and unflinching account of the highs and lows of one nurses life on the front line. A beautiful and shocking novel with a joyous ending that will make you both laugh and cry."

– J Alexander

Chapter One
A New Chapter

I woke up early, the heat already making me sweat. I looked at the alarm clock next to my bedside, the numbers flashing ominously on the screen read 5:00 am. I looked around my room for the very last time, the posters on the wall, my childhood books, sitting alongside my Nursing books. The few belongings that I owned, and my Gibson Guitar stared back at me, solemnly as if knowing that something big was about to happen. I felt sick my nerves, and fear of what lay ahead getting the better of me. Slowly I got out of bed and tiptoed, down the stairs. It was quiet, I couldn't hear my mom or dad. I opened the back door to let in some fresh air. It was going to be another hellish day; the sun was relentless. It was only then that I saw my poor mother, she was washing my VW Camper the floral design on the side glistening in the sun as the water dried in the hellish heat. I stood there silently watching her.

"Deme my love", come here, she called to me smiling. I have washed your van and filled the tank up. Let me help you pack your belongings. Holding back my tears I ran to her and hugged her feeling her slight frame beneath my touch. She was practically skin and bones.

I knew I would have to leave soon; I didn't want to let go of my mom, I wanted to hold onto her for a bit longer. I didn't know what I'd do without her, and for a moment I panicked and didn't want to leave. If I stayed in Greece, I could help her and look after her, but I knew it was a ridiculous thought, she was so proud of me wanting to study and travel I couldn't let her down. So I smiled and tried to look happy.

Before I drove off, I saw her wiping salty tears from her eyes, waving goodbye to me. She had hugged me and given me a thick envelope, informing me not to open it till I reached my new home.

She held me and said, "Make me proud, agape mou (my love)."

"I will, Mom; I promise to try."

The time was 12:30 p.m. Greek time, and also the last time I would see her alive; she was battling Metastatic Breast Cancer and had a few months to live; I didn't know that at the time, I would have never left if I had. But she had kept that secret well.

I felt like a furnace sweat pouring down my face, all the windows in the camper van were down, yet it was still sweltering. The back of my cramped van was full of boxes of clothes, books, and a huge hamper of Greek delicacies, for the long journey. My Gibson guitar slowly rocked back and forth; like a desert mirage it shimmered in the grotesque heat. It was unprecedented weather. So hellishly hot, Europe was on the verge of a mini meltdown, yet we were being assured that Global warming was not happening.

I drove for three more days. Finally, to exhausted to carry on, I decided to take a break to re fuel and charge my batteries.

I arrived at the beautiful historic town of Monte Saint'Angelo, in Puglia Italy. I was mesmerised, by this beautiful little town, the distinctive whitewashed houses glistening in the sun. The view was so breathtaking that I parked my van and just sat there, lost in thought, sipping my cappuccino taking photographs. I always knew Italy was beautiful, not as beautiful as Greece, but then of course I was biased. But beautiful non the less. Bella ragazza (beautiful girl), I heard someone shout, blushing I waved to the two teenage boys on their mopped, their beautiful faces and tanned skin glowing in the sunlight their carefree laughter could be heard as they drove off. Continuing my journey, I passed a kiosk to ring my mother. "Deme how are you"? I am in Italy mom, I miss you. "Deme my love I miss you too", but I'm so proud of you, drive safely and ring me when you arrive in England.

Finally, after what felt like a lifetime I was approaching Cale, heading for England. I felt bad about leaving my mother; she had looked so tired and weary when she had waved goodbye to me. She also looked sick, I couldn't quite put my finger as to what exactly I felt was wrong with her, and Sod's Law, I was just starting out in my medical studies, not coming to the end of them if I was, I would have easily spotted her symptoms for what they were. The weight loss, clumps of hair in the bathroom sink, vomiting, she had breast cancer and didn't even tell me. I suppose she thought she was protecting me, given the fact I no longer lived at home and was going to be studying in a completely different country. I wish she had told me before it was too late. Looking back, I had so many warning signs, from her asking about prosthetic bras to her enquiring about remedies to stop her vomiting. I would have done anything to have kept her alive I loved my mother dearly.

When I was growing up, I always remembered her as being this beautiful and elegant slim woman, with beautiful auburn brown hair always wearing red lipstick. She had a permanent smile on her face, always caring—I couldn't believe how carefree she appeared, considering what she had to put up with from my father. Where I loved my mother, my feelings for my father were an entirely different story.

I hated my father; he scared me, he hit me and called me names over the slightest thing, you little moron you'll amount to nothing! He was loud and nasty, and to my young eyes would appear menacing; also, my father was a horrible abusive drunk who gambled. When he was winning, he used to come home all happy and full of smiles throwing money around playing the doting husband and father; when he lost, we knew that the night would be a nightmare.

One such night, I heard him come in swearing and shouting, it was almost 2:00 a.m., and my poor mother was asleep. I heard him through the walls shouting at her calling her names; the slaps across her skin penetrated through the walls. I was scared for a five-and-a-half-year-old; things like this were horrible to endure. I remember getting out of bed as quietly as I could—I could hear my mother crying softly. I crept into the hallway and opened their bedroom door; I didn't really understand what I was seeing through that small door opening. I was practically a baby, and I found it strange that my mother was bent over the end of the bed while my father was standing behind her, grunting and groaning. I was a child, I just wanted to help my mother, but I could see the fear in my mother's eyes as she turned, spotting me at the doorway she mouthed, please, go, I'm ok. Many years later, I would come to the sickening realisation that my mother, the love of my life, had endured endless rapes and degrading sodomy at the arms of a so-called loving husband.

Back in those days, we didn't have halfway homes for abused women, and especially in Greece, things like this were most defiantly not spoken of. My mother carried on, as usual, playing the dutiful wife. She was a fabulous cook and used to make amazing meals feeding friends and my father's business buddies with extravagant dishes of moussaka and stifatho. Along with her amazing dishes, she was a great baker producing sweet cakes and chocolate full of glorious fattening calories. But she never put any weight on no matter how much she ate. I was so envious of her, I only had to look at a cake and my butt would expand in width. I didn't know at the time that she suffered from bulimia and was vomiting the food she was consuming. I didn't know why she would do something like that until I heard my father make a snide comment one day about how her ass was looking like a hog's backside, and she was disgusting. "No one will want to fuck you, looking like that," he sneered laughing, drinking his Jack Daniels.

So, in order to keep face and stop the neighbours talking, she started throwing up after eating. My poor, poor mother, why she put up with this, I'll never know. The saddest thing of all is that when he used to go on business trips abroad, he used to screw around regardless. I dread to think how many women he slept with or the brothels he frequented. I found this secret out by chance one day when I was taking the laundry to be washed. Something had slipped out of my father's trousers; it was a book of matches with what looked like an escort agency motif on the front; reading it, I found out that it said, 'Endless Sexual Pleasure'. I picked them up and hid them in my shorts pocket. I really didn't want my mother to find this out. I knew it would break her heart. My mother was a martyr putting up with my father's abuse till Cancer saved her by taking her away to hopefully a better place; this might sound horrendous, but sometimes death can be a blessing in disguise.

They say you shouldn't let your past determine your future, but my past is what drove me to decide to train as a nurse; I wanted to help people, be kind to them, offer support, and nurse them back to health. I wanted to make my mother proud.

These thoughts kept my tiredness at bay while I continued my journey through hellish heat to my new future.

Chapter Two
Hell

I had hoped that when I arrived in the UK that I would have a break from the terrible heat of Europe, but England was also sweltering; it was nearly 40 degrees, and for England, that was unheard of. The country was on the verge of a meltdown also, and everywhere you looked, people were huffing and puffing, eating Ice Creams, a carnival of colour, having water fights and generally enjoying this glorious weather regardless of the constant warnings from the government to keep out of the sun, England was not used to these hellish weather conditions and people were making the most of the glorious weather.

I, on the other hand, was sweating buckets, stuck in a traffic jam from hell, while the needle rose off the temperature gauge. This is what Hell must feel like! The congested traffic made matters worse there was a accident ahead, and the traffic had just about come to a standstill. I looked around me, people with fans and drinks, shirtless men with their beer bellies proudly on show, teenagers in swimsuits, having water fights, looking at the cars passing, not a care in the world. I turned the air con full blast to cool myself down, for a second, I felt dizzy, the heat was draining my energy and I felt like I was in hell, even with the windows down I was profusely sweating.

The world became hazy for a bit, my vision blurred, and I nearly passed out, thankfully, the traffic eventually began to move, and the sweet air came through the windows, the gentle breeze felt wonderful. I slowly continued my drive, the radio keeping me company, Madonna was singing, Lucky Star, the beat catchy and carefree, for the first time I felt excited and optimistic this was the start of my new life, and I was curious to see what it would bring.

I heard the high-pitched siren before I actually saw the Police car behind me flashing me to stop. I felt panic rising, my chest felt tight, my day was going from bad to worse, I don't know if it was good luck or sixth sense, but I instinctively reached for the envelope my mother had given me resting on the passenger seat and shoved it in the glove compartment, together with all the food wrappers and coke cans.

I pulled over and tried to look relaxed; the officer was in his early thirties, good looking with a kind face. "You do know your car is bellowing smoke?" which is highly illegal in this congestion.

What could I say—it was fine during my drive through Europe—nobody stopped me then, I didn't think that would have done me any favours, so I answered truthfully. "Yes, officer, I'm sorry, I'm on my way to the hospital, I'm already late," praying that he didn't arrest me, I'd lose my registration before I'd even started. I felt like crying, makeup streaming down my face, hot, sweaty and emotional; I didn't even look good enough to flirt my way out of this one.

My distress must have shown because, instead of booking me, he called the AA for me and waited with me till they had arrived. We chatted while we waited for them to turn up; he asked if I was excited about starting my new career; I said I couldn't wait, and this was all I had ever wanted to do; he looked at me sadly, which I found strange. He then said, "I was like you all eager and excited, wanting to help people, now all they seem to do is piss me off on a daily basis, and if they are not pissing me off, they are either suing or assaulting us. I hope your enthusiasm never leaves you, as mine has."

When the AA had finally arrived and thankfully fixed the problem, the officer wished me well and told me to "develop a thick skin; otherwise, the profession will either drain you or kill you." I smiled, thinking how very wrong he must be; nurses and doctors are there to save lives and help people; I had every faith in them and could not wait to embark on my exciting journey. I was very naïve and innocent; little did I know that years later, I would look back on his words with remorse and wish I had listened to him.

Chapter Three
Insomnia & Decorating

That night, when I had finally reached my destination, after a three-hour wait and a further two hours driving. I turned the engine off and looked up at the beautiful but slightly run-down Victorian terrace. It's architecture a polar opposite to the apartment blocks of Thessaloniki. I looked in the glove compartment for my keys, but they were not in there. I sat frantically searching for them for half an hour, to no avail. Finally, too exhausted to care, I parked the van outside, locked the doors and slept fitfully in the back of the van.

I woke up starving, sleeping in a camper van all night wasn't a great start to my new life, the keys ironically were in the glove compartment hidden out of sight. I was so exhausted from driving that I'd completely missed them. Thankfully it was Saturday and I had the weekend to unpack and catch up on some much needed sleep before I was due to start my induction at the Hospital on Monday. After I had unpacked my belongings from the van. I had a long warm shower, I was starving, I made pasta using the herbs, oregano, and feta my mother had packed for me in the hamper and took it with a tall glass of iced tea to the small, enclosed garden of my new home. I sat there lost in thought watching a little Jack Russell Dog running back and forth to its owners, in the park overlooking my terrace. I watched it as she ran around barking, bringing back sticks to her owners tokens of her affectionate nature, a lovely creature, loyal and loving, so unlike the people I had yet to encounter, barking happily oblivious to being watched.

After I had eaten and taken a long nap, I decided to empty the trash out of the van; I couldn't turn up on my first day as a trainee nurse in a filthy disgusting van. Gathering a large bin bag, I went to empty the crap from underneath the seat, and glove compartment nearly binning the envelope my mother had given me.

The gods must have been watching because I luckily spotted it before it went into an already full rubbish bag, shoving it in my jeans pocket; I worked slowly to tired to rush, and it was past midnight before I had unpacked and organised everything; it was only then that I sat down to open the envelope. What I found inside made me gasp, 50,000 Euros, I counted it three times uncomprehending what I was seeing, but I was right, 45,000 pounds, in crisp new notes with a letter. WTF??? I certainly wasn't expecting this; thank God I had hidden the envelope when I was stopped by the officer— imagine trying to explain this when I didn't even know it was there? Oh, sorry, officer, I didn't know it was money doh! I would have been spending the night in a cell for questioning—that would have gone down well with the university. Finally, when the shock had gone, I sat down to read the letter enclosed in the same envelope…

Dear darling Deme,

I hope when you finally get to read this that you are safe and have reached your new home to embark on your new exciting life. Please don't be shocked by the contents of the envelope, and please do not try to give it back to me. That money is for you; I spent a long time saving it, away from your father's gambling eyes. I want you to have it and spend it wisely, perhaps as a deposit for a new home—the choice is yours but use it wisely. I want you to have a happy, carefree future, and I am so proud of you for pursuing your dreams in medicine; I am so very proud. Don't forget your poor mother. I will always love you and will be watching over you, keeping you safe.

All my everlasting love x mum.

I wiped my tears which were pouring silently down my cheeks, unaware that I was even crying my mother's words had such a profound effect on me, I sat there numb, all hopes of sleeping now completely gone; I couldn't even ring her, it was too late, and the phone line had not been yet connected. I just sat there, windows open, in shock, feeling sad, and wishing I could hold my mother and tell her how much I loved her, wishing I had never left her.

I remember well the evening thunderstorms of that first summer of my new life; the nightly storms vast, yet beautiful, their rhythm a bass drumbeat, matching my own heartbeat in my chest.

I lay in the dark, listening to the rain, the fan a permanent fixture in my room, the low hum as the blades rotated keeping me cool. Planing out my exciting future that was unknown to me. I would doze on the bed, then wake to more rain, then heat, then lightning, eventually I gave up sleep and started decorating instead, one room at a time. Listening to the summer storms that were relentless but electrifying nonetheless, and in the endless days that followed, my insomnia completely took hold of me, like a vampire it started bleeding me dry making me restless.

Chapter Four
Autopsy

We were silent, and unprepared. Nervously standing in small groups, it was during our second week as trainee nurses, we stood staring at the naked dead body, not really knowing what to think, or do. My new friend Joy stood next to me; we were in the same cohort. She was a foreign exchange student from Dubai, a slight wisp of a girl, 5'1, with dark chestnut hair and big, beautiful blue eyes, she looked as petrified as me, on the verge of tears. We wore our new trainee nursing uniforms—all pressed with shiny new fob watches and lanyards that had our name and rank on them. First year nursing students—expectant and eager, taking things in—all smiles and awe, some of us still wondering how the hell we got to the stage of newbie nursing students.

Our hands and uniforms were clean they had not yet been stained by the blood, of patients or of their bodily fluids. Our hearts had not yet been contaminated with the horrors we would encounter in the years that followed. Horror's that we would have never imagined, and sadly as we continued our studies would never forget, the people I would treat, the violence I would witness, and the sheer atrocities of human nature had not yet left an impact in my life, looking back I now realise how lucky and naïve I was, I was so young. I felt a little nauseous, trembling just a little, my arms had erupted in tiny goosebumps. We chatted in our small groups, some of the student's nervously cracking jokes, then fell silent, feeling a little sick, as the instructor knife in hand began cutting into her body. Until that day, I had never seen a dead body in real life, I felt a little faint, bile rising in my mouth; I hoped to God, I didn't embarrass myself by puking up all over it. I bit my lip hard, tasting the blood in my mouth, while I stared at the corpse on the table, all the while trying to focus on the mottled dead body, pretending it wasn't real so that I could deal with it.

She was 37 years old, I stared transfixed at how perfect she seemed even in death she looked alive, her skin translucent. She was so young. I was horrified, I couldn't believe it when the instructor took the medical drill to cut round her skull in order to remove her brain, peeling back her skin exposing the skeletal frame and muscles beneath. I stared at him unable to comprehend what I was seeing I caught my breath unable to breath. Coming from a sheltered Greek family, I had never witnessed such things. Her body was riddled with the Cancer which had eventually killed her. The feeling of death felt almost palpable in the closed stuffy room. It's deathly essence lingering even after the lesson was over. They say curiosity killed the cat; I didn't have to volunteer to feel the tumour, but I was curious and eager to learn— touching it, observing its deathly purplish tinge, the hard 5 cm deadly lump in the lecturer's hand felt alien, it had been silently growing inside her eating her up and spreading its deadly poison.

The thought that my mother had also succumbed to this end, suddenly hit me, causing me to panic. The feeling was strong and frightening, I had to hold back my tears. We worked tirelessly, slowly reducing her anatomy to pieces. I felt so sad to think that she was once a real human being, one who once had dreams, hope and life; She had two young children that would grow up motherless, they were only three and five, what an age to lose your mother. In the last week, as we placed her once functioning organs, heart, Lungs, brain into bags for research, the lecturer asked if anyone would like to feel brain. I raised my hand I was eager wanting to learn, funnily enough, I had always thought that it would feel rubbery for some strange reason, however when I touched the pink bumps it felt solid and hard, never had I ever envisioned myself touching a human brain, I held it in my hands, it felt heavy and surreal, it just goes to show how our choices in life, open us up to endless possibilities, and whole new experiences. Touching the brain, and watching the instructor stitching her body back up, and placing her in a body bag, I had a vision of my mother being placed into a similar bag, I finally lost my composure, I felt sick, it just felt so final, death the end of a life, I felt overwhelmed and I no longer felt able to function my hands started shaking. I had a severe panic attack it hit me like a dose of salts.

Joy watched silently as I ran to the nearest exit, just about making it without passing out. Ironically my years of watching horror movies, somehow didn't prepare me for this. I ran outside and promptly threw up. Sitting there on the steps next to the mortuary of the University Hospital, I tried to regain some form of compose. I looked out across the lush campus that stretched out for miles into the distance the clock tower clearly visible, it was such a beautiful campus. I sat looking at the edge of town and at all the students busy rushing to classes, life going on as usual. While the life of a young woman in her prime lay deceased behind me. I thought how utterly cruel and unfair life was, I sat for a bit longer knowing that I should go back inside, this was highly unprofessional, and I felt like a wimp, embarrassed. I sat on those steps crying silent salty tears, when I heard someone approaching. It was Gianni, the good-looking Greek consultant, that had every nurse and doctor swooning over him. We had become friends because we both came from Greece, and as I could speak fluent Greek, we had started talking in Greek whenever we had to work together, cracking jokes and talking about our country and the beautiful weather, which drove all the other nurses green with envy.

Gianni was model smouldering good looking.

"I'm ok, thanks; I spoke trying to overcome my embarrassment let me freshen up in the rest room, I need to wash my face and I'll be there in a minute."

Placing his hand on my shoulder, he said, "It's always scary this baptism of fire, but you will eventually get used to it; if you ever need to talk, my office is always open." He handed me his card with his extension on it. "Please talk whenever you feel the need to," he said, his hazel eyes kind and helpful.

Three years later, I was nearly graduating and on my last placement as a student nurse, I would soon be becoming a full-fledged registered nurse. It was nice to know that Gianni had kept his promise and had my back. I didn't know it then, sitting crying on those steps, but he would become a lot more than someone to talk to; I didn't know it at the time just how much my life was going to change, and how the eventual circumstances that would unfold would alter my life beyond my wildest dreams.

Chapter Five
Accident & Emergency

I remember my first day as a newly qualified nurse arriving at the A&E department with a bittersweet mixture of nostalgia and pride mixed with a serious amount of dread. To say I was terrified would be an understatement, even though I had finished my management placement and was very competent, had passed all my exams, and was given a glowing reference from not only my mentor, who was the sister of the Neurosurgery ward I had worked on prior to qualifying, but also one from Gianni. I was nonetheless petrified. I no longer had the security blanket of the title student nurse anymore; this was it, real world, here I come. I felt nauseous and a little excited. I was greeted by Annabelle, the kind-looking Sister of A&E, who would also act as my guide and preceptor during my transition from student nurse to staff nurse, she had a kind face which eased my anxiety a little. "Hello, Deme," she said, "it's a pleasure to have you join the team; if you're ready, which I'm sure you are, let's start the tour of your new home," she whispered. "We also have military personnel joining us in training for the month, so please excuse everyone running around like madmen trying to show them around."

So, it began—my tour, I was led to the front entrance. The Emergency Department has two entrances. Pit Stop, where a seriously ill patient has been brought in via Ambulance. And the main entrance where the walking wounded go to when they visit the ED. She explained the layout of the department and the different stages of how a patient was triaged. She then led me through to the main waiting area, it was so busy that people were sitting on the floor waiting to be called, it was utter chaos. The area is called the main wait area Annabelle said, trying to look calm as she manoeuvred through the crowd, of patients. I noticed that Police officers were also dotted around holding onto their prisoners waiting to be seen by nurses, Security Guards and the Mental Health Liaison Team could also be seen nearby. I observed the poor HCA's running around ragged taking observations & giving out food and refreshments like tea and coffee, sandwiches and hot meals. Years ago, you were lucky to get a drink of water, how things have changed. I looked around at the poor souls who had been waiting for hours on end. It was very busy, sometimes dangerous, noisy and hectic, I watched in horror as one patient tried to punch a poor health care assistant, he was so intoxicated or drugged up, and looked very pissed off at having had to wait so long to be seen. I silently followed as Annabelle led me into another area, trying her best to sugarcoat the chaos, by this time everything seemed to merge into one another, the noise and chaos giving me a headache. I was so tired having had so little sleep. She led me through to the resuscitation area. It was very flash and expensive looking with the latest observation equipment and computer systems. She pointed to a red phone on the wall, "That is your patient's lifeline; you will hear it going off constantly, and when it rings, you answer it no matter what; that phone is someone's cry for help, their chance, between survival or death." On the wall just above the phone were the words 'We are Here for You' I found out that this was the 'mission statement' there are a lot of mission statements dotted around the hospital, a feel-good vibe about them, to offer the public something to focus on when visiting, a sense of excellence and spiritual uplifting.

Years later, to my jaded heart, I came to the realisation that no matter how uplifting the messages, the reality is something entirely different. And for those on the front line who have to deal with cutbacks, Doctors striking and shortage of nurses and Health Care Assistants, the reality is far from jovial, but the amazing hard working staff grin and carry on. But I was new, and everything was wonderful in my eyes; I felt proud and eager to help people and make them better. When she had finished showing me around, she then led me back into her office to give me my new starter pack and go over my rota, on the way to her office I could hear the sister raising her voice saying to someone on the other end of the phone "You promised us a bed hours ago!"

I looked around the room, so many Police officers, I remember when I first started my training, there was very little sign of security guards or Police evident. Now sadly for everyone's safety, there are burly looking security guards dotted around everywhere, in case you get assaulted, stabbed or threatened. I call them public sector bouncers; in fact, I wouldn't be joking if I said I have seen fewer bouncers in nightclubs, the way times have changed is quite scary.

Heading towards her office we had to pass through the resus department. The resuscitation room is exactly that; basically, you are deemed so unwell that you are at serious risk of death and need urgent intervention, people who have fallen and have heart issues or bleeds on the brain tend to need the resus area. It was full of nurses and doctors, and a lot of high-tech equipment. It is an area where there are lots of beeping machines and ones that let out sinister hissing noises; this room consists of seven cubicles with hi tech observation machines, resuscitation crash Trolley and a unit containing ECG equipment, venipuncture apparatus, and a whole assortment of bandages and different equipment, on many occasions, it is, unfortunately, the last room a really sick person will ever see. I hope that the hissing and beeping doesn't terrify them too much as the next port of call is, sadly, the mortuary via the viewing/grieving room, the adult resus department, is also next door to the children's resuscitation area, and there have been times where consultants and doctors have ran out choking back tears, its heartbreaking as we all know that something horrific has happened and that child didn't make it. This really affects me and plays on my thoughts for weeks on end, my heart breaks for them, it's one of the worst parts of the job, nobody should lose a child. This private viewing room for someone who has sadly passed away, is a small side room very discreetly tucked behind the weighing platform, blink and you will miss this room, which I suppose gives the patient in it and their family privacy away from gapping stares and ridiculous people trying to capture things on their phone.

Annabelle said to me "It's a very important role; I'm sure you are very proud," I nodded, taking everything in I was silent my tiredness had taken over and all I wanted to do was go home and sleep, but I smiled and followed her as we continued the tour, the Sister then explained the different coloured uniforms various staff wear, so many uniforms in different colours, worn by different ranks, from the Student Nurse uniform to the New Nursing Associate, the HCA, to the Nurse etc.

I have often seen the bewildered look on patients' faces when they hear this, and I feel very sorry for them; it must be mind boggling to come to grips with the different people looking after you.

As we finished the tour, she showed me where the staff room was, and where the various Doctors offices are situated; they can be seen dotted along a narrow corridor, tiny rooms you can hardly swing your cat in. They act as the consultants' rooms, and HR rooms, far too many to be counted with wooden plaques outside each office with the names of the various consultants and Doctors. There were also framed photographs of members of staff who had sadly died through Covid.

Then finally, she led me to a little enclosed garden for staff use. I very rarely had the chance to use this beautiful garden as I am always too busy to have a break or too knackered, but it was beautiful and tranquil and was built through the kind donation of a patient's family, it was built in honour of a deceased family member.

This was to be my new home for the next three years, one that woke me up and started to give me thick skin. One where I shared good news and bad news with patients, laughed and cried, felt euphoric and angry, and contracted a whole load of viruses in, a department in which I witnessed some unbelievable things, some things which have haunted me to this day. A fairly large department that left an even larger impression on a new expectant and happy newly qualified nurse.

Chapter Six
The Crying Room

It was 3am, the witching hour as it's superstitiously called. It was a Friday, I remember the day and time as if it was yesterday, I was in my second year working in the A&E department, by that time I had started to develop a thick skin, on this particular night you could hear the emergency bells going off their high beep a continuous siren. I was still tired, but I stumbled out of the makeshift bed I was resting in, in the departments staff room, other staff members on their brake were sleeping in the relatives' room, anywhere we could find that was quiet so that we could take our much needed half hour break laying on hard chairs to tired to care about comfort, we all ran to the resuscitation department to attend to the emergency. The room was full, a blur of blue scrubs as the consultants and nurses ran around her. I was shocked there was so much blood. Her face was so badly beaten up that she was unrecognisable. She was only a young girl. Miraculously she was alive, desperately trying to sit up on the trolly. "I'm freezing," she cried, weak and disorientated, I grabbed a warm blanket from the blanket warmer and wrapped it around her. Doing everything I could to offer her a little comfort. The doctors had tried to insert a cannula in her arm, but she had repeatedly removed it in her, delirious state, I assisted and tried to calmly hold her hand so they could finish the job, "Where is my mother?" She was screaming. "I want my mother!" I held her gently and tried to comfort her, your mother is waiting outside, don't worry let us help you she was manic and in shock.

Her injuries were horrific, she had cuts along her arms, two horrendous black eyes where she had been punched, a broken nose, and a split lip, dried blood was matted in her beautiful long blonde hair where she had her head repeatedly smashed with a blunt object. I watched as Gianni remove his gloved hand from behind her head, it was, slick with blood she desperately needed a transfusion she was losing a lot of blood, her pulse was very weak. By now she was fading in and out of consciousness, she needs an urgent CT now he shouted where are the porters? We moved quickly our time precious, someone called the blood bank for two units of blood, when it arrived, we quickly hooked her up, she was given medication and pain relief, and plenty of sedation we all worked on autopilot doing everything we could. Her injuries were terrible, I don't think any of us seriously expected this girl to survive.

Looking at the slides, we could see the extent of the damage done to her brain. The CAT scan images rose, one after the other, on the computer screen, their black and white images showing the extent of the damage. The consultant looked closely at the subdural bleed clearly visible in her brain. Mr Jones, the head neurosurgeon, was there, and he stared at the screen. He spoke to the junior doctors in his calm manner, explaining the images, to them. Turning to me he spoke quietly,

"Deme, please go and find the family, they need to be prepared for the worst, we will do our best but this young girl is not going to survive. I looked at him, unable to speak, we all knew that she probably wouldn't make it, her injuries were far too catastrophic. I felt sick to my stomach as I approached the room, they were waiting in."

I softly knocked on the door, feeling sick and briefly hesitated before I entered, my heart was pounding. The family were huddled together in the relatives' room, the mother pacing back and forth. The room is small, off the corridor of the busy department. Sparse with a couch and a chair, with a single window facing the University campus, in the distance I could see a large blossom tree, ironically it was in full bloom, spring on its way, the beginning of new life. I've never really grown used to going into the relative's room, having to either break devastating news or good news no matter which department I have worked in, the room is always the same, small and impersonal. I hated this part of my job, I felt like the Grim Reaper, never really knowing what to say, fearing the complete devastating effect my words would have on the family members.

A newly elected Pontiff, when he changes from his cardinal red to the papal white, will often go to what is known as the Crying Room. A room where many have gone to pray for courage, faith and to confess any sins. He will also no doubt pray for endurance to fulfil his duties as best as he can. It is a huge responsibility and a rite of passage. I often think of the relatives' room as the hospital version of the Crying Room. Where news of hope, life and death is discussed, and those who enter and leave that small sparse room receive news that will either break them or give them a little hope. Either way, they will never be the same again. Their lives will have changed forever in one split second.

"Are you Carol's family?" They looked at me, the mother, father and a younger man. "My name is Deme," I said as they sat there motionless, wanting to know the prognosis. I didn't look at them too closely. I couldn't bare to look at the pain in their faces. I was tired, fatigue taking over after the long hours and relentless heartache I witnessed on a daily basis. This particular shift had been extra hard. We had so many patients to see, the backlog of ambulances waiting to offload their patients, we couldn't treat people fast enough, we had so little time to see them all, we were all exhausted, they kept coming in, an endless stream of walking wounded, becoming angry at having to wait for 16 hours to be seen, along with an alarming rise of mental health patients, having nowhere else to go. I couldn't believe how busy the department was and had come to the bleak realisation that the world as we knew it was a strange place; The choices we make in life can either make us or like in Carol's case break us.

"Please," the mother begged, "please tell me how she is, how bad is it?" She was a petit 55-year-old, with blonde hair, the lines around her eyes made her look older than her years, her husband towered over her a gentle giant holding her trying to offer her some comfort as she was almost hysterical, her eyes were hollows in their sockets.

"We'll know more in a few hours," I replied. "She has sustained a really bad traumatic head injury. It's an extremely serious injury, we are doing everything we possibly can to help her. Nick, the consultant, will be with you shortly; I will be the nurse looking after her; if you need anything, please do not hesitate to come and get me, she is in the resuscitation department everyone is doing everything for her, I placed my hand on the mothers back trying to offer her support, I didn't know what else to do, I gently offered her a box of tissues to wipe her tears."

I felt like a failure not having done enough to help her. "Is she going into surgery?" the brother asked, choking back tears, trying to be brave for the sake of his parents.

"We are waiting for her CT results," I said, she has had a blood transfusion and is currently sedated. Just then there was a soft knock on the door Mr Jones the neurosurgeon walked in with Nick behind him, their faces solemn. I instinctively knew Carol had lost her battle and didn't make it before they even broke the devastating news to the family. I didn't know where to look; the pain and anguish on their faces broke my heart. Carol had sadly passed away the trauma to her head was fatal and the bleed had eventually killed her, everyone had done all that they could to help her, it was too much they were unable to save her, Nick had tears in his eyes as he gently spoke to the family, I had read the shocking report – her fiancé had repeatedly hit her with an iron, it was over a petty argument the damage she sustained was irreversible.

The mother's screams were deafening and could be heard down the corridor, No! No! Please no! My baby, my little girl! Her screams penetrating the walls in the small room, the father started swearing, shouting, "That bastard! I told her to leave; she wouldn't listen." He was throwing furniture around, making his wife cry more. I pleaded with him to stop; I could understand his grief, but security wouldn't be as understanding. I begged him to consider the other patients who would be petrified listening to his grief; I felt awful saying this to him; God only knows how I would have reacted if I was told the same news. He eventually stopped when the brother tried to calm him down. When he had finished sobbing uncontrollably, he wiped his eyes...

He turned to me and said, "Her fiancé Robert did this to her they had been together for one year, we never knew he was abusing her from day one, we even laughed when she showed up with a broken nose, claiming that she had walked into a wall, she was known to be clumsy, how would we know??? The bastard has murdered my baby girl, my beautiful baby girl. He rang 999 then jumped of a bridge I hope the prick is dead!!! The police haven't even caught him, so now he doesn't even get justice; how fucked up is that." Why??? What did she ever do to deserve such cruelty. I already knew all this as the police had informed me upon her arrival. The fiancée was 21; she was only 19, just a young girl, just starting out in life. She was a graduate in Fashion and was about to start a new job as a junior designer in London, her whole life lay ahead of her. Now because of this monster she was dead.

They had cleaned her and changed her blood-soaked clothes, she had a clean hospital gown on, her arms folded across her chest, the doctors had stitched the laceration on her face, the wound a jagged scar stretching from the edge of her brow down her cheek to her mouth, Nick had done his best, matching up the creases of her skin, the wound stood out, an ugly raised worm, upon her delicate features.

I looked at Carol even in death she looked like she was sleeping, the nurses had worked hard to clean her cuts and bruises they combed her hair doing their best to make her presentable for her family, she looked peaceful; the family waited to see her, my god what a difference 48 hours makes I felt sick; to think that 48 hours ago, she was going about her day, whatever that day had in plan for her, she was breathing, walking, talking. Forty-eight hours later, she is peacefully silent, the machines and ventilator that were keeping her alive now silent, I wondered what sort of life she would have had, the Catwalk shows she would have attended, jet-setting around the world, showcasing her amazing Shoe Designs, 19 years old such a waste. I went to get her family, watching the father fumbling under the white sheet covering her, he gently lifted her body burying his head close, it's not really her it can't be, his sobbing broke me, I gently closed the door behind me, hearing the sobs as both the mother and father held onto her, rocking back and forth. They say it takes on average twenty attempts before a victim of domestic violence finally plucks up the courage to leave their perpetrator. I sometimes wished that those being abused realised the danger that they are in sooner rather than tragically later, that the monsters they are with never change, they just manage to camouflage their coercion and violence from others extremely well. But sadly, I know love is blind, and they are so brainwashed by these evil bastards that they don't see the reality, or in many cases don't get the support they need sooner. It was early morning nearly the end of my shift. I eventually went to the nurses' station for shift change. Feeling sick and devastated for everyone who had been involved, I felt deflated that I couldn't do anything to save her. We all did, Gianni, the surgeons, everyone involved; it was a draining night, one of many I have encountered over the years.

Her brain had swollen uncontrollably, cutting off its own blood supply, eventually killing her. What a tragic unfair end to a young life, why? I couldn't comprehend it.

"We are supposed to help people." I could feel my voice rising on the verge of losing it, as I handed over tears welling up in my eyes, why couldn't we save her.

"She is on the donor register," Gianni said as we stood there listening. "Are the family aware of this? I'll talk to the family this morning."

Great, so now we were taking care of her organs. I felt deflated; I knew she was the best of donors, that was obvious, she was young, strong, and undamaged in every other way what was beyond recognition on the outside, was thriving and perfect internally, she had the ability to save a life, with decades left in her heart and lungs, and kidneys, in her eyes and liver.

I looked around the room she was in, the family had left, but had brought in cards and flowers, pictures, and belongings they sat lovingly arranging them around her, their grief must have been unimaginable, yet they had done this a shrine to their daughters' life. I looked at the photos a young child on the grass laughing, another of her holding a new-born in her arms smiling. I looked at Carol, peacefully laying on the bed, awaiting the mortuary attendants to come and collect her. I hoped that she could see what her parents had done, and the love that they had for her. I also believed but never mentioned this that perhaps the patient is aware in some strange way that these personal belongings are there around them, I had read that people sometimes have outer body experiences and can see what's going on around them in time of trauma, but I never voiced these opinions, back then people would have thought I was mad. I gently closed the door behind me I felt overwhelmed. This would have been the third patient in a week to have succumbed to the violence of a loved one. I could feel myself detaching, becoming drowsy, I needed sleep more than anything, I was working such long hours—a new patient had come in. I had to go and do a quick set of observations and set up her paracetamol drip, gathering her medical history, I prepared her medication and inserted her cannula before I went home.

Chapter Seven
Dog Bite

I love my job, and helping people, that's what drove me to train to be nurse, there are very few people I don't go out of my way to help and to do my best to offer them comfort and support in their time of need, however there are some evil people who make my skin crawl, and I do find it hard to keep a non-judgemental attitude. This was the case of one particular patient. She was in her fourties', she had been brought in after suffering life changing injuries to her face. I watched her from afar she was reading a magazine, her hands bandaged up. Her mouth was held together with a multitude of wires and screws. Bruises and cuts, clearly visible in the early morning light the white sutures holding them together, like tiny threads glistening. I approached her, slowly, trying to avoid her gaze. She needed her medication as she was still in a lot of pain. I introduced myself, and she looked at me, good morning, I said trying to sound cheerful though inside I could feel my anger rising, I knew that I had to act in a professional manner without being rude or judgmental, but it was hard so very hard.

"Do you have any allergies, to morphine?"

"No."

"Do you have any other medical problems, like angina or diabetes?" She shook her head; just give me the damn medication she mumbled incoherently almost seething.

I had read her medical notes and circumstances of the injuries, the nurse handing over to me still had tears in her eyes, she was an animal lover like I was. I felt sick to my stomach. Shaking slightly, trying to control any form of emotion and treat her like every other patient, I held out my hand with the little plastic pot of morphine. Taking it, she looked at me and tried to talk again, but was unable to due to the wires and brace holding her jaw in place. Taking the pen and paper on her bed she wrote, where's the bloody surgeon, when am I going in for surgery. I have paged Dr Crawford to review you, she is on her way down. Seeming satisfied she screwed the paper and threw it on the floor for me to pick up. Her name was Joan she was 43 years old, she had been discovered by the RSPCA officer, after they had broken into her flat. Somebody had tipped them off after hearing dogs whimpering and crying. Inside they had found ten severely malnourished animals' three of which had died. Vomit and dog excrement had filled her filthy flat. In cages puppies were crying, limp and terrified. The RSPCA officer was so traumatised that he threw up. Pieces of her flesh had been found on the floor where the poor starving creatures had started to gnaw at her while she was sleeping. Her screams had alerted the neighbours and they had called the police.

The morphine had started to work by the time Dr Crawford arrived and Joan was asleep snoring loudly. She looked at my face and could see that I was about to lose my composure, my eyes were red, and my tears were silently flowing down my cheeks. "Deme sweetheart why don't you go for a break, we are taking her up to theatre, as soon as the porters arrive."

I didn't need to be told twice. I just about managed to make it to the toilet in time, as I proceeded to throw up my coffee and breakfast, I sat in the small toilet cubicle sobbing uncontrollably. I am normally very calm and don't get upset easily, but unprovoked cruelty to animals and children, hit a very raw nerve and break my heart. The rest of the day went in a haze. I treated my patients, smiled and wrote my nursing notes. But all the while what kept going through my mind was the image of the poor starving creatures, which ironically due to the severity of the abuse and bad treatment had to be put to sleep. I hoped to God the evil bitch suffers, I hoped that every time she looked into the mirror and saw her grotesque deformed face, that she is reminded of her appalling cruelty I hoped that she would be banned from keeping animals indefinitely. I couldn't personally comprehend it, and to this day reading her notes and remembering the graphic details of the case still gets me extremely angry.

That night I went home and sat in my small garden, the moon shone brightly, the firefly's dotted about left a magical glow in the air. I was unable to sleep, and instead sat for hours crying silent tears, tears for all the poor animals, that didn't have a voice, tears for the abused women I treated, the disfigured children that had been neglected and hurt by the people who we're supposed to care and love them. I cried for the cruelty I witnessed daily. Humanity at its very worst. I didn't know how much more I could take, before the horror's I witnessed on a daily basis started to take their toll on my mental health. I sat and prayed to God to give me strength to keep calm and carry on.

Chapter Eight
Keep Your Mouth Shut
and Eyes Covered

Everyone who works in the NHS and the Healthcare profession is made aware of the serious occupational health hazards involved. It's always very advisable to wear the protective equipment and gloves, plastic aprons and goggles provided in every trust to stop pus from boils, blood, vomit and pee as well as diarrhoea from being ingested either by the mouth or travel via the eyes, or open cuts. Bodily fluids tend to have a mind of their own and can hit you where you least expect them to. Don't ever assume that it won't happen to you like I did on this one particular occasion.

It was 9:30 a.m., and the last patient I was seeing as I had just finished a twelve-hour night shift. I was supposed to go home at 8:00 a.m. but we were waiting for the agency staff, and they happened to be running late, and because I like helping my department out, I volunteered to stay that little bit longer.

The patient had come in for an operation and needed a cannula inserted in his left hand. I gathered the cannula, saline and needle needed to do this. Preparing everything correctly is paramount, so is wearing your gloves, which I did. What I didn't do, however, as advised, was wear the plastic goggles—I wasn't being lazy, I just couldn't find any, and I was so tired that all I really wanted to do was insert the cannula and catch the next bus home. I was nearly finished trying to position the bung in place when all of a sudden, from nowhere, blood started spurting from his hand, and not in little amounts it went everywhere straight into my face, going into my mouth, eyes and nose. I tried to remain professional throughout, I finished inserting the cannula while my heart was pounding in my ears; I then grabbed some wet wipes and made myself presentable while I went to one of the other nurses to ask her to set up the drip.

I then ran as quickly as I could to the nearest toilet, found the sink and disinfectant and started washing my face like a madwoman, panic rising, feeling a bit sick, after I had washed till I was red raw, I went into the toilet and threw up. Shit, shit, shit, fuck! I had two choices: when this happens, and it involves blood, either a needle stick injury, or like me blood going directly into the mouth and eyes, you are advised to have the PrEP medication which can stop HIV from taking hold and spreading throughout your body however you have to have to take it within a 72 hour time frame. Currently, there are only two FDA-approved medications for PrEP. PrEP is prescribed to HIV-negative adults and adolescents who are at high risk for getting HIV through sex or injection drug use or in my case work related contamination.

The drug of choice during this scary time is called:

Emtricitabine/Tenofovir-disoproxil/mylan, it comes as 200 mg/245 mg film coated tablet. It is highly effective when taken as indicated.

The once-daily pill reduces the risk of getting HIV from sex by more than 90%. Among people who inject drugs, it reduces the risk by more than 70%. The second is to inform your line manager immediately after the event. This is where I didn't know what to do; how was I going to explain that I didn't use the goggles provided; I felt so stupid.

I decided before I went home to go to the GUM health centre and explain what had happened. I knew that I would be given the drugs I needed. If that failed, I could go to my local GUM clinic. On my way to occupational health, I had a terrible thought, what if someone that I knew saw me? I was, of course, thinking highly irrationally, and I was tired, nearly in tears and overthinking everything. The thing that kept coming into my mind the most was what if the patient was HIV positive; I mean, you never know, do you? Then that means I, too, could have been infected. I didn't have time to waste procrastinating; I ran instead as fast as I could to catch the bus to my nearest GUM clinic, remaining anonymous.

I was luckily given the tablets I needed and followed the strict guidelines, I had to have regular blood tests, which terrified me. I spent the next six months panicking, I couldn't eat or sleep, I was petrified. It was a very stressful six months; I was a complete wreck. I lost nearly three stone worrying, it was horrific; all of this could have been avoided if I had worn my goggles. The most ironic thing was I later found out that the patient had no prior STDs. Irony at its best, but you never know. Years later when the deadly Coronavirus came along, I was even more vigilant than most, and wore the protective garments constantly unable to breath during long 14-hour shifts, but my brush with blood and the fear and anxiety it had caused me had taught me a lesson I would never forget.

Chapter Nine
Contagious Laughter

She sat there waiting patiently to be seen, her arm bandaged up in a temporary sling, before she could have an X-ray to assess the damage done. Her long brown hair pulled into a high ponytail softened her features making her look younger than her years. She was holding her young child in her arms, trying to read to her, both of them oblivious to the chaos around them. It was the beginning of my shift, and the ED was once again extremely busy, the department was buckling under the strain of having to treat the nearly 560 or so patients who had visited in the last 48 hours. Unprecedented numbers and some of the patients where very angry at having had to wait long hours to be seen. We were short staffed, and the junior doctors and nurses were running around haggard trying to treat everyone in a timely manner the HCA's comforting patients and offering them drinks and food. I was at the nurse's station preparing a saline drip for a patient, engrossed in the task at hand.

I could hear them both laughing as they read the story, I looked up and for a brief moment I was transfixed watching her lovingly stroking the little girl's hair. She sat laughing at the pictures in the book, her giggles could be heard throughout the department. The nurses and doctors near by saw me watching her and they too stopped to look. Her little giggles and shrieks of joy were so infectious, that I watched in amazement as the people around her, also started to slowly smile and begin to interact with her. For one magical and surreal moment the ED was transformed from the usual chaos to the sound of laughter. The little girl was-unaware of the effect she had on everyone around her. The sheer magic and her ability to briefly heal and make people forget their problems, it was a magical moment, one that made the doctors and nurse's smile. Then the porters arrived to take her mom for her X-Ray, and the magic disappeared as they were wheeled away. It was a moment that has over the years stayed with me. A moment that had the ability to heal my heavy heart, children and animals are so innocent and understanding. Her laughter reminded me of a time when I was a young child, visiting the fair in Greece, I remembered the hustle and bustle as we ran through the crowded amusement park, my best friend Betsy leading the way holding my hand so I wouldn't get lost. We'd run as quickly as we could to ride as many of the fairground rides humanly possible till we had to go home. Stuffing our faces with Hot dogs and Ice Cream, making ourselves feel sick. Our laughter could be heard for miles, and like the little girls, made everyone around us smile. It was a magical time, one that I can clearly remember, these magical moments in life are few and far between, it's a shame that sometimes as adults we forget magic exists.

Chapter Ten
The Assailant

She had just arrived back from the operating room; I was working a bank shift in the burns department, Holly lay in her bed in the bay opposite the nurse's station, I saw her while I was writing my nursing notes. She was awake and alert. She had bandages covering her torso arms and parts of her face. The morphine drip attached to her cannula dripped silently offering her temporary relief from the excruciating pain that she was experiencing.

The attack had happened a month earlier, she was getting into her car; when out of nowhere an assailant approached her and threw acid all over her, we were not aware of the full circumstances, but word was going around that it was a jealous ex boyfriend, she had broken up with him and he wouldn't accept it. The acid had burnt the left side of her face, damaging her eye, part of her nose and lip, her back and arms were also burnt, she had wandered, screaming, bleeding into the street, a grotesque sight in a panicked daze until one of her neighbours saw her, and luckily, acted fast and poured a two litre bottle of milk over the burns, he kept going inside and bringing out pan after pan of cold water, washing her skin trying to wash away the harmful chemicals, he did this till the paramedics arrived and brought her in screaming in clear shock. She was about 30. They'd operated all day, excising pieces of her undamaged body to make a graft the best way they could, a draining procedure and a lengthy one. The plastic surgeons working hard to salvage her skin, they took parts off her shoulder blade, and her lower back that had luckily not been damaged by the acid, with the muscle still attached the surgeon carefully cut it, to make the best of a new jaw the plastics team working tirelessly for hours on end. She needed extensive surgery, and this was, the first of about thirty surgical procedures. The plastics team also performed a Tarsorrhaphy, in order to preserve the damaged eye, they completely closed it, joining the upper and lower eyelids. Her damaged eye was going to remain closed for an extended period of time not only to protect the eye from infection, but to also allow the cornea to heal properly. Her mother was constantly nearby crying hysterically praying, stroking her hair, unable to comprehend what was going on. They tried their best to fashion a new mouth; they tried to make her lips. She was a modern-day Frankenstein, it was awful to watch, I felt so sad for her, looking at the photos around her the ones her mother brought in for comfort, showed a stunning looking young woman, she had just been offered a Modeling contract, and was going to host a new TV show. But her ex boyfriend had completely destroyed her life, now she lay in her bed bandages up totally unrecognisable what was her deranged boyfriend thinking? what horrors must have crossed her poor mind the pain, she must have endured. It was an unimaginable tragedy, all the staff were shaken and mortified. We all rallied round her, helping her, giving her pain relief. Her mother had set up a go fund me page to help with future surgeries, and we all put as much as we could afford into the fund. Amazingly within a month the fund had raised thousands of pounds, people from as far as the states were donating. Thankfully with the amount raised, she would be able to have the best possible treatment and plastic surgery. When I first started my nurse training we were given a lecture on the benefits of Leech therapy. Watching the slides in the lecture room I never thought in a million years that I would actually see the benefits from this procedure in real life. Leeches are used to attach themselves to the damaged skin tissue, they are able to release a local anaesthetic which helps to reduce the pain at the site of the attachment. The amazing little critters also secrete a substance that helps to open up the blood vessels, which helps to reduce the pain at the site of attachment, natures very own vasodilator, they also secrete hired in, and Calvin that work by thinning the blood. The leeches are attached to the affected site for 15 to 60 minutes. After the leech has dropped off, blood drainage from the puncture wound continues for up to ten hours. Leech therapy was discussed in length with Holly's family members and Holly herself, she looked horrified at what we were proposing, but agreed to go ahead.

So, it began a small colony of leeches were placed on the affected skin on her face and damaged areas of her body, they stuck there like small little black vampires feasting, sucking salvaging her tissue, performing their silent miracles. Thankfully, she couldn't see them or feel them, these little leech vampires were very important.

They drained congested blood from her wounds, allowing it to grow healthy, nowadays new wound management and modern technology have come along with far superior results, but the leeches performed their miracle and occasionally are still used. The skin remained a pink colour as long as the leeches did their work. They would feast on the wound, swell up, then drop themselves like fat pregnant worms onto the bandages, then the damaged skin would gradually begin to darken again, turning dusky with blood. It was my job to help with attaching them onto the skin, I would reach into the container, picking new leeches with tweezers, carefully so as not to drop the squirming little creatures, little worm vampires until they latched onto her skin, sucking, sucking, growing fat miraculously helping her skin to heal. Holly was eventually moved to a private hospital in the States, the Go Fund me page had surpassed everyone's expectations and the amount raised was phenomenal. We received a big thank you card with a big bunch of flowers, and a photograph, Holly was unrecognisable, the surgery she had received was phenomenal, she was beautiful, she still struggled with her eyesight, and a lot of the burns on her body were still very sore looking, but on the whole she looked amazing. I was so very happy for her. But the leeches must have left an impression on me because in the months that followed, I slept fitfully—I was being chased by vampires but in the dreams, they were giant black leeches, with blood-filled red eyes screeching, bits of flesh dripping off their teeth, sucking, chasing after me. I went back into work the next morning, to start a new shift, and I must have looked terrible because Gianni took one look at me and offered to take me out for a meal after work. "Dee," he said, "you look pale and so thin, go home for the day, I'll sign you off sick. And later tonight, let me take you out and try and fatten you up a bit; I'll pick you up at 9."

I tried to protest but he was having none of it. I could see some of the nurses raising their eyebrows, smirking and whispering behind my back; I took my uniform off, hung my lanyard and badge in my locker and said, "See you at 9, then, outside the Bell tower of the medical bloc at the front of the Hospital." When I arrived home, I just about managed to lock the door behind me, feeling dizzy, tired; I fell into my unmade bed, uniform still on, too tired to change and within minutes, I was asleep.

Chapter Eleven
Chaos on the Frontline

It was the middle of a long wrenching 12-hour shift, what I like to call the witching hour as it seems. Before the end of each shift, we always seem to get an emergency call; I was knackered, my date with Gianni had to be cancelled I had completely screwed up as it was ridiculously busy. I had forgotten that I had booked a last-minute graveyard bank shift, which pissed me off to no end, but I had to grin and bear it, my mum's pride and memory was on the line; thankfully, I had slept well, roughly nine hours. *That should last me for the gruelling shift ahead of me*, I thought.

It had been non-stop for the last four hours. I was treating a little old lady who had fallen in a care home that had been short-staffed and broken her wrist. The poor lady had not only waited three hours on the floor for an ambulance to turn up, but now needed the added pain of having it manipulated and pulled back into a more manageable position. Though this procedure is quite common in the ER, it is quite daunting for the patient and very painful. I was giving her more pain relief, when the 'red phone went off'. A man was being airlifted with serious burns. I had no option but to apologise and hope that the medication I gave her offered some relief before she was seen properly. Had I said this to a younger patient, all hell would have broken loose; the elderly I have found are very resilient and accept on most occasions what they are told. "Don't worry, my dear," she said. "I'm sure there are more important people than me; I don't mind waiting."

My heart broke; I had to explain that we were very short-staffed, and due to staff striking there were only a few doctors in the whole of the ER I looked into her kind eyes full of pain and my heart broke, care homes piss me off no end, they never seem to give the care they promise, as they are always short staffed, and the majority of the time badly run, the owners too busy lining their pockets. When I arrived to meet my new patient, I had underestimated just how bad it was. On close inspection, we could see that most of his body from the neck down, was a mass of red ugly blisters and white swollen skin. He was screaming in agony; we gave him strong pain killers and plenty of fluids. We were waiting for the surgeons to come and assess him. Mr Ford's burns were very bad, we worked tirelessly cleaning his wounds over and over again with cooled tepid water and moist gauze. Applying cream and ointment to help decrease his pain and prevent infection, if not treated properly Mr Ford's burns would cause him chronic pain, disfigurement and leave terrible scars. We worked tirelessly it took hours to apply the specialist dressings. Everyday for weeks on end we dressed and re dressed his burns. We did everything for him, poor Mr Ford, he never complained. When the plastic surgeon came to see him, he stood closely looking at his skin, touching areas, assessing the necrotic dead grey colour, which wasn't blanching the damaged nerves underneath completely dead, even when pressed hard, there was, no reaction in Mr Ford's face.

I felt awful for him, he was so very brave. I had only seen this form of necrotic skin in an elderly lady once before. She had developed a severe pressure ulcer, the worst I had ever seen, she was a little 90 year old lady, she had been bed bound for a while, and she was brought into hospital for treatment, we initially assessed her and checked her over we were all mortified when we removed her incontinence pad and found a gaping hole in her coccyx it was big enough to fit a small fist in, it was horrific, so bad that we contacted the safeguarding team to investigate the case. Mr Ford's injuries were just as horrific. Though Mr Ford was only 55 and strong, we knew right away that it would be a matter of touch and go. "It was a gas canister," he said, "at the school; it was faulty, he said as he lay there."

"Everyone at the small village school is praying," I heard one of the Auxiliary nurses say, "it's all over the news, caretaker remains in critical condition in hospital and may require reconstructive surgery, after suffering severe burns in an explosion at a school, no one else was hurt." Our thoughts and prayers are with the family.

"All I remember after that," he said, "was the fire and flames."

Dr Christa introduced herself to him, speaking softly explaining everything to him, what she was going to do, the procedure involved everything. He listened quietly, nodding in agreement. Christa was 5'3, with chocolate brown hair, and big beautiful brown eyes, she looked like a young version of Marina Sirtis from Star Trek. She was kind and helpful, all the nurses and surgical interns would go quite listening to her every word. Dr Christa was very intelligent and kind, and above all, she was very skilled. She was a master in her field, and widely respected, having written articles for The Lancet and a Bestseller. She was originally from Athens, and often tested the junior doctors on Greek medical words, it used to make me smile because I knew what she was talking about, because I had the advantage of speaking the language fluently, we became friends and often spoke in Greek, sometimes swapping recipes, she was an amazing cook and used to bring food in for the staff, laying out the dishes in the staff room for us to enjoy, she was so kind.

Dr Christa was an exceptional plastic surgeon, and she loved a challenge.

Dr Christa was ready; she stood in the room in her blue theatre scrubs, quietly inspecting the gleaming sterile instruments laid out on the table, chatting to the medical students watching, waiting, arms folded as we brought Mr Ford in. I thought it was miraculous that he'd made it this far alive, but he was a tough cookie and wouldn't give up. Staff were working round the clock, pouring an ocean of fluids into him; giving him Opioids to help ease the excruciating pain he was in.

Burn surgery is simple, the main principle is to remove all the necrotic tissue and to preserve the viable dermis in the wound bed. This procedure is called a Tangential excision, and Dr Christa was an expert in this field. You basically take a straight razor to the burns and shave down through them until you strike live tissue, you can see the thousand tiny little bloody pinpricks as the blood rises, from the flat surface of the wound, they also give hope and the possibility of recovery. She operated, engrossed in her work talking to her surgical students "You want a bed of severed capillaries, so that they can rise to the grafts, and help the new skin grow." She explained while she worked, sweat forming on her brow under the theatre lights. "But you also need good skin to perform the graft, to start with and it was very obvious, Mr Ford didn't seem to have much good skin left."

Christa examined him thoroughly and started with his inner, untouched thigh. It was my job to assist her; I monitored his observations and hung up another bag of fluids, the anaesthetist was behind his sterile drape monitoring Mr Ford, soft music could be heard playing in the background Christa liked to have music playing as it helped her concentrate while she worked her miracles, I also liked listening to it as it was very relaxing, and soothing. She was an exceptional surgeon the way she was able to find the proper angle, her fingers on the blade slicing through Mr Ford's skin. I watched the skin rising, off her blade. It was a time-consuming process taking her long hours and it was exhausting for the surgeon. But Christa continued, delicately salvaging his skin, hunched over him while her delicate hands, sutured away, grafting the new skin trying to make Mr Ford look half human. She so loved her work, and she allowed the surgical interns watching, to look at the process through the microscope, unlike the other surgeon's she had the time and effort to talk and train her students.

As Mr Ford didn't have enough good skin to cover all his burns, so we had to wait for his grafts and skin to heal. Performing this procedure time and time again; the skin healing for us to come back again, slicing through it once again, bandaging and re dressing the wounds the labour of love and many weeks, leading into months. But he was a jolly patient man, who, though in pain, used to make everyone laugh. I was feeling rather low and I especially appreciated his banter; I had been working solid shifts for months on end, trying to save money, and I was tired, but at this point, I still loved my job and wasn't yet put off by the rumours circulating the wards regarding members of staff being struck off or referred to the NMC how ironic this would be as further down the line I would lose my good friend because someone who had nothing better to do had referred her to the dreaded NMC.

"It's going to work; he'll take time to heal but thankfully he's going to make it". Dr Christa said, the smile on her face said it all. We had all prayed he would pull through.

When he was awake, Mr Ford was reading a magazine on motorhomes, his bandaged hands fumbling through the pages, he smiled at me when he saw me, and when I mentioned that his wife was here, he smiled and told me to bring her in, I rearranged his pillow, and went to fetch her. His eyes shone and he was smiling.

"Are you going to buy a motorhome?"

"Yes, been thinking about it for a while, after this near-death experience, hell I'm definitely going to buy one, it's going to be a surprise my wife has always wanted to travel, perhaps a long road trip across America, it's something I have always wanted to do, life is far too short! They had discussed it between themselves. They had decided to sell everything they owned and travel the world, after nearly losing me, she wants to enjoy every moment with me. We are taking our young grandkids with us; it will be a new adventure. The accident could have been avoided you know; my solicitor is looking into it; I could be due a good compensation package. Either way, I won't be able to work again, so it's a sort of early retirement gift to myself, he showed me a beautiful picture of the lavish motorhome, the price was staggering but it was gorgeous."

"You go for it, I said smiling it's wonderful that you are doing this,". I can only imagine what he must have felt like when the canister went off, the flames, and hellish heat, the pain. I was in awe of him; he was so optimistic and didn't give up regardless of what he had endured. He was also determined to live this new life after his brush with the grim reaper. Ironically many years down the line I would also have my brush with death, and only then did I realise what a wake up call it can be and could fully understand Mr Ford's zest to live life, to the max, life is short and very precious.

His wife was waiting to see him outside. He winked at me and said, "Bring her in." I went to fetch her; she was 48, with mid length red hair, and a beautiful face. Her name was Sheena, she had brought in a big box of chocolates for everyone to thank us. I watched her as she stood by her husband's bed. They were both smiling and even though he looked like a mummy all bandaged up, the ugly bluish-red leathery mess of his skin, where his grafts grew like something out of a horror film, even through all this horror they were optimistic, they were oblivious, far too busy plotting and planning their new adventure, they were like lovesick teenagers.

A few months later, during handover, Dr Christa, happily said, "They have done it the house is on the market, she was excited, coming from a large Greek family she loved travelling visiting her relatives dotted around Athens. I looked at her expensive Loubutin shoes on show the red sole visible. This was her second love—designer shoes, and she had a vast collection which he showcased whenever she was on rounds like prized medals all in wonderful colours and designs you could hear her heels in the corridor. She was currently also commissioning a new and upcoming young designer from Nottingham to hand-make her next pair, costing a staggering £650, but she was good, and after having shown her designs on the runway of London Fashion Week, she was highly sought after, Dr Christa loved the next big thing.

"So, she continued operating it went on for weeks, the weeks flowing into months, Mr Ford with his patient wife by his side, being operated on in the hot room as Dr Christa stood there with her razor, her forehead damp in the heat, her bright, eyes questioning the junior nurses and doctors with endless questions and stories. She so loved her work and to this day will always be a source of inspiration to me, she made me smile, this amazing Consultant with her kind eyes.

"Everything happens for a reason do you believe that Deme? I believe that Mr Ford and his wife are going to have a bright adventurous future what do you think?

"I do Christa, we smiled at one another,"

We found out many months later after Mr Ford had been discharged and recovered, that they had been successful in selling their home and were now travelling across the United States they were currently in the Florida Keys, the glorious sun cheering them both up and helping Mr Ford heal. They had sent in a big bunch of Chrysanthemums and a lovely card with a photograph of them both standing behind the beautiful backdrop of the Grand Canyon, they looked relaxed and happy, the card full kind words, expressing how grateful they were that their hopes and dreams had been fulfilled and blessed and that we gave them hope, that the staff, nurses and doctors were all knights in shining armour; they couldn't thank us enough. I looked at the beautiful bouquet of flowers they were Chrysanthemums, the flower symbolising hope. I smiled and felt humbled; we don't often get stories of happy ever afters or many thanks from patients, it's mainly complaints and referrals these days, but when we do, the kind words and gratitude, they stay in our hearts and memories, and we feel appreciated, I will never forget Mr Ford, and his zest for life, he was an inspirational bloke.

Chapter Twelve
A Series of Unfortunate Events

The room went quiet as she walked in unannounced during the MDT meeting, we heard that we were getting a new consultant but as yet only a handful of us had met her. Eva was gorgeous, she was petite with blonde curly hair, voluptuous lips and a knockout figure. Everyone called her Ms Monroe due to her uncanny resemblance to the real Marilyn, and when she smiled her features lit up and you became captivated by her beauty. She was new to Orthopaedic Theatres, having only been with the department for a few months, but she was rumoured to be an exceptional surgeon. She had recently transferred from London St Guys, having been given a brilliant reference, Gianni would serve as her mentor while she got acquainted to the way the department ran. I wasn't jealous because I trusted Gianni, he said he loved me and wanted to move in with me. I believed him and knew he would be an amazing mentor he was brilliant at his job.

Eva was calm and polite, but she could also be demanding and hot tempered especially if things set her off. I remember someone saying that she once threw an instrument across the room at a young scrub nurse, for not listening to her. The poor soul ran out of the room sobbing. No one dared to question her, because her face would go still, and her beautiful features would change, and the look on her face would make you tremble. She thought she was invincible; and when she was angry used to terrify the poor junior doctors and scrub nurses, but she used her good looks to her advantage manipulating those around her with her charms and could worm her way out of trouble. Eva was an extremely gifted surgeon, there was no doubt about that, it was no wonder they called her beauty and the brains. She was quick, and accurate, and could suture a wound so well that the scar looked almost invisible, she was in a league of her own, able to perform intricate surgeries that far outshone her male contemporaries. There was a lot of jealousy, and the nurses and junior Doctors would either love working with her or hate it.

Then several months later, Gianni told me that she had handed in her notice and just like, that she was gone, vanished, the wards and corridors were full of hushed rumours, something about a Only Fans Page involving one of her patients, that particular patient had also referred her to the General Medical Council, as he wanted more than what her fan page was offering, but no one really knew the truth, just a lot of gossip circulating about. Eva had handed in her notice, she was unable to practice in the UK, till her investigation was over. I couldn't believe it, another brilliant surgeon gone. I was curious as to why someone who appeared to have everything, would risk it on a stupid platform, but you never really know what length people go to for an extra buck. She was apparently raking in quite a lot of money each month from her side hustle and had purchased two properties abroad. I didn't see what the problem was, what you did in your spare time was your business, but I suppose the GMC thought it brought disrespect to the profession, and wanted to investigate the matter further. I would miss her, and unlike everyone else could relate to her quirkiness. She had taught me a lot, Gianni, was distraught complaining that the department was wrong to let her go. It shocked me at how upset he became.

I remember once during a long day shift, I was working with her in theatre, passing her the instruments while she operated. The anaesthetist invisible behind his drape. A man was laying on the table, prone with his lower back wrapped in the sterile blue cloth. Looking closely, I could see the tumour it was horrific and located in the most perilous position. Wedged between the lower lumbar region of his spine, compressing his spinal cord, causing him excruciating pain. The tumour was bulging, under pressure, it looked alien and surreal, I watched her, as her small hands delicate in their sterile gloves deftly operated, engrossed in her work, her floral perfume, in the air mixed with the metallic smell of the instruments, slowly excising the tumour bit by bit miraculously without harming the spinal cord and surrounding nerves. She successfully removed that tumour, it was unbelievable, the theatre staff were mesmerised by her ability. In the background you could hear Ozzy belting out his hit track Bark at the Moon, the air in the theatre charged and intense.

"Thank you, guys," for all your help tonight she said as she was stitching up the wound, "Nurse Deme, can you take this to pathology please." I stepped slowly behind her, being careful not to touch the sterile area. There sat the tumour in a sterile pot on the trolly, it was quite a big tumour it looked alien pulsating; it reminded me a little of the movie *Frankenstein*.

She had miraculously saved this man's life, he had to spend a month on the spinal ward and needed extensive rehabilitation to help him walk again, but he lived, and his prognosis was good. Eva's surgical ability was outstanding, she was a brilliant surgeon, I couldn't believe what Gianni had told me, how could she be gone no longer with us! I hoped that whatever became of her, that she was happy.

A few months after she had left, I was going for a much-needed coffee break. I was tired and didn't really want to talk a lot, so I sat back quietly pretending to be engrossed on my phone. Gianni came and sat next to me looking clearly distressed. What's wrong? I asked not really wanting to know. But he looked so shaken up that I felt sorry for him. Deme you won't bloody believe what I have just heard, he was rubbing the back of his neck a gesture of nervousness, by this point I could read his body language, rolling my eyes I thought what's gone off now. Mr Lewis the plastic surgeon is fighting for his life on D3, they say it was suspected arson or something like that. But you will not believe this he said, whispering so that he couldn't be heard. They have arrested Damian, in relation to the attack. I couldn't believe what I was hearing. Everyone knew the ongoing feud between them both, it had been going on for years. Damian had tried to Whistle blow on the poor professional conduct of the surgeon, and the department as a whole, and the powers that be in management didn't like it, they tried to silence him. He was suspended on full pay pending a full investigation and made to sign a document saying that he wouldn't disclose the details of the investigation to anyone. It had near as damn it ruined his once brilliant career. He lost everything, his marriage, his home which he had to sell to pay his wife, everything gone. His hatred for Jack Lewis, had grown to the point of obsession. He had planned the attack carefully over many months. And on a dark blustery evening had taken cover in Jacks vast Garden, crouching low so that he wasn't seen. The petrol hidden in a black container by his side. He waited patiently for Jack to come outside for his customary cigarette and then threw the petrol covering him all over. He ran off leaving Jack screaming in agony as his wife had manically tried to put out the flames, but the injuries were very bad. He was now fighting for his life on D3. The police caught Damian, on the way to the house because he was speeding, and he was arrested so now to top everything off he was facing a lengthy stretch in her Majesty's pleasure. His once brilliant career was gone, all the good he had done and the lives he had saved, forgotten. I looked at Gianni, he looked drawn and sad. I sat silently drinking my coffee not really believing what I was hearing. I thought how simple my life was when I was a child without this craziness, could anything else possibly go wrong, it was front page news, Jacks grainy picture was on the front page of every newspaper throughout the country, his philanthropic work and long career over, his life and that of his family completely destroyed.

Chapter Thirteen
In Shock

It was a just a normal day, no different to all the rest. At 7:00 a.m sharpe the charge sister came in to handover from the night shift. Behind her two Police officers followed. She looked visibly upset and was trying hard not to cry. We sat in silence wondering what had happened. I am very sorry to inform you all that our beloved sister Annabelle, is no longer with us. The gasps could be heard as we clutched at each other grief stricken and in shock. For those of you who didn't know her Annabelle was a well loved and respected member of our team. She was known for her kind heart and compassion. Tragically last night on her way home from work she had collided into an oncoming car instantly killing the family and paralysing the child in the back. She never made it home; her internal injuries were too catastrophic, it wasn't her fault, the car in front didn't give her enough time to manoeuvre around it. The Police officer stepped forward to explain what had happened as the sister ran out of the room sobbing. Annabelle after completing a 12-hour shift with no breaks, had been too exhausted and shouldn't have driven home, instead of taking half an hour to rest before she left, she instead wanted to get home, she was tired and the car in front had stopped suddenly, she wasn't paying attention to it and crashed right into the back causing the catastrophic chain of events. I'm afraid I have further bad news. For those of you working in the Children's ED this morning I need to make you aware, that you will probably be treating the child involved in this horrific collision. We will be getting specially trained staff in to help those of you who need that extra support or counselling. We were all in shock, this should have never happened. Someone screamed we are too bloody short staffed!!!

This is all wrong, I have had enough, she said running out of the room crying, some of the other nurses ran after her trying to console her. We were silent for the rest of the handover. I looked around the room, my eyes blurred from crying. I just couldn't believe it. The rest of the day went quickly, the departments usual banter with the patients, gone. We were all too upset to be jovial. One patient who wasn't aware of what had happened drunkenly said, "oh what's wrong with your miserable faces, has someone died". I was mortified and couldn't wait to finish my shift. Walking home that night I looked at the stars twinkling brightly in the sky and felt such a profound sense of sadness that I had to stop and catch my breath. Why are so many bad things happening I thought? it's almost as if the world was completely an alien place, how can Annabelle no longer be here, she was due to give me my appraisal this coming week, she was happy and had just become a grandmother, I couldn't believe it, none of us could. Just a random cruel event that was out of anyone's control, could the accident have been avoided if Annabelle had left a few minutes later? Maybe if she had asked for a lift and not driven home this wouldn't have happened, if the driver in front had not stopped. There could have been so many different endings. I silently prayed for Annabelle's soul and for the family and young girl involved, I would miss Annabelle, she had been so good to me when I had first started in the department. The following week we held a silent vigil in her memory, staff had blown up a photograph of her and it sat in a beautiful gold frame in the staff room, flowers and cards by the bagful had arrived far to many to display, so instead we put them in an album, for staff to read and remember her by.

Chapter Fourteen
Easter in Greece

When I was a young girl during the school holidays, I used to visit my father's family in the small village of Mouryes, and every Easter, whole communities would come together to light candles—the traditional customary gift for Easter is the 'Lambada' (Easter candle) which is lit during the midnight service of Easter Sunday. The exquisitely unique Lambada is a gift given by godparents to their godchildren. We used to visit my dad's village, on the rare times he didn't drink, and gather by the dozen in the small church to pray, give thanks, and wish for good fortune for the coming year. The children showing off their own unique candles and gifts from grandparents.

As the village overlooked the sea, I could see for miles, the candles and lights shining from each adjourning village, the warm air caressing our cheeks. My mother holding my hand telling me to make a wish, she looked beautiful her dark hair flowing over her shoulders, her red lipstick glistening in the soft glow of the candles flame. That time had imprinted itself in my memory, the soft prayers, the smell of incense, the beautiful vast blue green sea, without visible edges, full of twinkling candles entering the distance till they burned out, like falling stars, people's wishes being answered. A small constellation of human need, dreams and prayers to the Greek gods for a second chance, health, and happiness, so much emotion in one night. I also remember my mother quietly wishing for happiness and an end to my father's drunken abuse, she thought I couldn't hear her, but I caught every word, and I too silently prayed, I prayed that he would leave, find someone else, for him to disappear and leave us for good.

Chapter Fifteen
Bleeding Heart

The man was blind drunk, he was a large bloke, and wore black jeans with a leather jacket, the jacket had the most beautiful image of a gold phoenix on the back, the gold stitching intricately woven, he was full of slurred half formed words and threats, watched nervously by the other patients sitting waiting around us. Someone could be heard vomiting. Another was demanding to be seen after waiting for 16 hours. The usual chaos and mayhem, "My God! I don't know how you work down here," Jo said. She was working a bank shift and couldn't believe what she was dealing with. The drunk man could be seen thrashing his arms trying to hit the poor nurses and Auxiliaries helping him, security had been called in and, for once the old method of restraint was used, they held him down on the trolly, they had no other choice, the nurses ran round him, a swarm of blue scrubs bending over him trying to give him sedatives trying to calm him until he was quiet, he could be heard spitting and swearing , the veins on his neck standing out from the strain.

Two young homeless men were being given hot drinks and something to eat, the urine and vomit on their clothes leaving a terrible odour. The other patients looked uncomfortable and were politely covering their noses with hankies. It broke my heart to see these poor souls, who knew their circumstances, I think one of them was a homeless veteran I recognised him from his past visits. This mortified me, imagine serving your country and ending up homeless! It was all wrong. After I had completed my drugs round, and had a few moments to spare, I went to the cupboard where we keep spare clothes and clean towels and gave them to the two homeless gentlemen, leading them to the shower room so that they could get changed. I wasn't really supposed to do that as the ED isn't like a ward, we don't really have the time or the manpower, to offer showers, I know it's a sad state of affairs but I needed to do something. I couldn't stand to see them suffer watched by others. Humanity and compassion shouldn't have a price tag. I knew I was in for a telling off.

The sister called me over, Deme you are a wonderful kind person, but we can't help every bleeding heart, she snapped, I wasn't offended by her harsh words, I knew she was so stressed with having to juggle everything that she took it out on me. Sorry sister I won't do it too often I apologised. Now go back and triage those patients, we have a major incident coming in. Gathering the observations machine and notes I hurried off not wanting to give her anymore excuse to reprimand me. A few hours later I saw them both with hot drinks and clean clothes, they looked tired but at least they were clean and dry, and now well fed. I smiled and felt happy, that we had at least done something to make a difference even if it was a small difference.

Chapter Sixteen
Christmas Cheer,
Tea and Biscuits

Over the years, I have grown accustomed to working either Christmas or New Year's Eve. This has been a regular occurrence for the past six years. This year was no different; it was Christmas Eve, and every year, working the night shift is absolutely crazy. The A&E resembled a Third World War zone, Police, door security all working their hardest to restrain aggressive drunks. Nurses caring for vomiting patients and underage teenagers, domestic abuse victims coming in with swollen faces and broken noses being triaged and sadly with nowhere else to go, having to go back home to their abusers. All of society's problems rolled into one night, and they came in droves non-stop chaos. It was only 9:30 p.m. when he came out of nowhere oh bitch, I have been waiting here for 10 hours what the fuck! Are you going to treat me or what? I had just finished triaging a really poorly patient. I looked at him, he was about 45–50 he had a swollen face, a black eye and his lip needed stitches, he reeked of alcohol, and looked like he was about to hit me, if I didn't see to his immediate request. Please be seated sir, I will be with you in a few minutes, I want to be seen now he slurred coming closer almost in my face I need my methadone. I felt panic rise in me, I had to keep my composure. Please just let me get your details and I will be back. I led him to one of the cubicles as he was already starting to scare the other patients. Please sit down or lay on this trolley and I will come over to you once I have your file, would you like a drink of water? No just fucking hurry up with my methadone. I walked out and drew the curtain then went to the nurse's station and looked for his file, I felt uncomfortable, I didn't know if I should notify security, but I gave him the benefit of the doubt, and decided to just treat him. Great night this was going to be. I had literally been at work for an hour and a half, and already I was on my sixth emergency, having patched up the drunk in the cubicle, who now had a security guard watching him, somebody had already notified security and they were watching him, he was starting to scare the other patients. A young girl had come in with about four of her friends, she could hardly walk, had a graze on her knee ripped tights and her skirt looked like it had particles of vomited kebab on it. I took her into the bay to take her observations and to find out what had happened, though it was more than obvious.

"What happened?" I asked quietly.

"Been drinking, she could hardly talk, Vodka, Blueberry flavour yummy," she slurred, then without notice, she proceeded to vomit, directing it unintentionally towards me. It went everywhere on my shoes, uniform and hair. The plastic apron thankfully stopped further damage, but only just. Thankfully the HCA that was assisting went to get more vomit bowels and help while I went to change my uniform.

When I arrived back, I was informed that the 17-year-old was sleeping it off and did I want to contact the parents, I decided to take her observations before I went to ring her mother, I felt something wasn't quite right with the young girl, I don't know what made me think this, but I had a gut feeling, that she had something more seriously wrong with her than her presenting alcohol abuse. Checking her observations, I noticed she had a spiked temperature, and upon close inspection I also noticed she had a rash on her hands, and they felt rough like sandpaper. I was worried and decided to get a second opinion from the consultant on duty. Jonathan was the on-call consultant that evening, and he also looked puzzled. Deme let's do a blood test and send her for a X Ray please. By that time my mind was mentally going over her symptoms, she was young and even though meningitis had crossed my mind, something else also occurred to me. I went over to her friend, who also appeared drunk but not as bad as my patient. I felt embarrassed but I needed to ask the question. Hello, my name is Deme, your friend is going for a Xray, so that we can get a more accurate picture of what's going on. I do need to ask a question though; it wouldn't be your friends time of the month by any chance, would it? The friend looked at me like I was mad, but thankfully answered me truthfully. I ran to find Jonathan. I found him looking at her X Ray, I think she may have TSS, from Tampon use, but it's only a thought I said. Deme, I think you might be right he said, pointing to her X-Ray on the screen, we could clearly see not one, but three Tampons lodged inside her vagina, I couldn't believe it, no wonder she was feeling so poorly. We had to move quickly, I set up an antibiotic drip and fluids. Deme, please go ring her parents, she will be stopping in we need to remove them,

Jonathan said. Off I went to wake up the poor mother. As I imagined her mother was beside herself with worry and was nearly hysterical when I said I was calling from A&E. "Is my baby dead!" She screamed, nearly deafening me.

I managed to calmly explain that no, not dead but she needed to stay in to be treated for possible TSS, would she be able to come to the hospital to be with her. I went back to the young girl and retook her blood pressure and temperature, in order to get her prepared for surgery.

Oh dear, the poor girl, I don't know what possessed me to ask about TSS, but I am so glad I did, I really hoped that she would get better, and that we had caught the infection on time. I felt so bad for her. I went to notify her friends, who also appeared very distressed by that time. What an awful way to end a night out with friends. The rest of the evening went quite quickly, I went back to see if the poor elderly lady who had arrived at the start of my shift from a fall, had been triaged, but sadly she was still waiting to be seen on the trolley in the now overfilled department. To think that a 92-year-old had to wait on a crowded corridor, scared and in pain really infuriated me.

I looked at the time 2:45 a.m. I decided I needed a break, a very overdue break. At the canteen, I ordered two sandwiches and two hot sweet teas. I then went back to find the little old lady. I spent my lunch break waiting with her sharing a sandwich and drink, I also covered her with a warm blanket. She was a delightful soul, who told me stories from her time spent in a concentration camp, and of how she lost her husband to ill health a year ago; "he was 96 years old and the love of my life," she said. Finishing her sandwich, she held my hand and thanked me for the time I had taken to sit and talk to her, her pale blue eyes full of kindness, "We don't get spoken to a great deal in the care home I am in; everyone is always too busy running around to spend a little time to say hello. You are a wonderful nurse, my dear—kind and thoughtful, thank you for the sandwich let me pay you, I was mortified and told her I didn't want the money, I just wanted to help her, and the sandwich was free."

I shook her frail hand, her fingers bent from the crippling arthritis and told her it was a pleasure meeting her, "I will really try and get someone to see you as soon as possible, I really wanted to help her, I didn't want her to wait any longer."

She smiled and said, "Whenever you are ready, that's fine with me. I'm warm enough, and all this hustle and bustle is the most excitement I have had for years; I don't want to go home yet; let me see a bit more of life."

I was stumped for words; all I could manage was, "I will try to get someone to treat you soon." I walked back towards the triage bays, and it struck me, the quiet and calm, I looked around, the majority of the patients had now either been treated or had left on their own accord; I gathered my thoughts in those few calm minutes, I felt deflated how could this be happening a 92-year-old lady, in pain having to wait so long to be seen, but it's not our fault, we have so many people to see, that the waiting times are now getting longer and longer, this is putting a great amount of pressure and strain on the poor staff who only want to help and do the their best for our patients. I stood their, waiting in my clean scrubs and apron watching her sip her tea, and eating her sandwich, I was tired, my eyes sore from lack of sleep, and I could feel a headache about to start.

It was 4 p.m already, the shrill ring vaulted us all back into action, we had a serious trauma involving two young boys, from St. Ann's, the estimated time of arrival was 15 min. The only handover we had from the paramedics was that it was a serious traumatic injury, from an altercation in a nightclub. The first boy to arrive was, beautiful but tragically very badly beaten up, a deep cut to his head, and horrific black eyes, his split lips forming a grotesque smile, on his face. He lay there his body involuntarily moving in spasms, his sapphire eyes half-open, he had a clear plastic tube sticking out of his mouth, the paramedics still trying their hardest to squeeze air into it through a blue rubber bag, we set up drips, and pain relief and called the blood bank for urgent blood, a haze of green scrubs working frantically to try and save him.

The younger of the two paramedics looked shocked as she spoke, "He's arrested," meaning his heart was not beating. As I turned away, I noticed his hair, blond, a bright band keeping his long fringe away from his eyes, his beautiful ivory skin smooth, he was so young his whole life ahead of him, I watched as his body heaved while the peddles tried to shock him back to life. We all heard the loud beep as the monitor showed the inevitable single flat line of his heart as his body gave up. One of the doctors ran out of the room her sobs could be heard in the distance. He lay motionless his beautiful eyes staring into the unknown. My hands shook as I covered his body with a sheet. A life taken away by a random act of violence.

The other boy was still fighting for his life, they wheeled him in, and we began: IV needles into his arms, observations, monitors beeping, everyone rushing to save him, then the sudden gushing waterfall of red spilled onto the floor, the monitor wires to his chest, voices rising, we were all rushing to save one life at least, I noticed he was blue, barely breathing. Taking the laryngoscopes, putting the blade into his mouth, I immediately felt how deeply unconscious he was, his muscles up resisting and soft. He was bigger than the first teenager, with a tattoo of an interact crucifix on his neck and two tear tattoos on his cheek, his close shaved black hair on one side smooth—the other side, a mop of curly hair—matted and red, full of clotted blood and white pieces entwined like little worms. It was only a few minutes later when I went to lift his eyelids to check the pupils for a set of neurological observations that I felt the back of his head, it was soft and squidgy, warm to the touch, withdrawing my gloved hand, I saw it covered with blood, hair and bone fragments, instantly I pressed the emergency button. Turning the head over carefully, we all saw the large gaping hole in his head.

Looking up, one of the nurses mouthed, "Jason's family are in the relative's room, waiting. Will you go talk to them?" By that time, Gianni, had arrived having heard the emergency buzzer going off.

I knocked on the door, and quietly stepped inside the room. They stood there, embracing one another waiting anxiously for an update. All eyes turned towards me, hope and fear intertwined, "Hello," I said, "my name is Deme, I have come to update you on Jason," they looked petrified. Gianni stood next to me, "I am the triage nurse that first treated your son; this here is the neurological consultant."

"I'm sorry, but your son is in a critical condition; the consultant is seeing him now," Gianni said, "I will update you further when I have assessed Jason."

"How bad is it?" The mother asked, half rising from her chair, her trembling legs unable to hold her body.

"It's bad," Gianni said. "I'm sorry; I think you should all be prepared for the worst."

She fell back into her seat, unable to comprehend what she had been told. Though Jason looked a lot older when I saw him, he was only 23 years old, "This can't be happening," she said to herself, crossing herself silently praying.

"Is he dead?" the father, a burly good-looking older version of his son, asked. "We heard that our boy, might be dead, say that isn't true, they only went out in the last minute to celebrate a friends birthday, how can this be happening!"

Gianni's pager went off as I was about to answer; the look on his face said it all.

"I'm so very sorry," he said, "but I have just had confirmation from the neurologist; I'm very sorry, but your son didn't make it, the wound was too deep, the damage irreversible." The room once deathly quite erupted, the presence of great tragedy manifested in shrieks of heart-wrenching sobs, the mother rocking back and forth, her crucifix in her hands flashing in the light, her husband trying to console her, looking into the distance, over my shoulders to a horizon only he could see.

I looked at the clock, 5:45, the break of a new dawn, I looked outside the world was waking up, the headlights on the passing cars shining like beacons, the blossom on the trees announcing the arrival of spring, another day about to begin. I went to the nurse's station to write my notes, a huge weight in my heart. I looked up at the sign above the nurses' station.

Keep Calm and Carry on, the letters on the sign read.

Chapter Seventeen
To young to Die

Deme, can you take over my patient Sandy one of the nurses handed me her notes, I have to go to resus. I looked at the notes and felt sick. I knew the patient from the numerous other times that she had been admitted. She was well known to the Mental Health Team. She had tried numerous times to end her life, from paracetamol overdoses to slashing her wrists, she was a regular visitor. My heart sank, I felt gutted, this particular patient hit a raw nerve, and I felt extremely sorry for her. She was only 17 years old, had numerous scars all over her arms and legs, from where she had been cutting herself, tonight they had found her on the car park roof, she was ready to jump again, screaming at the Security officers to leave her alone. Security had eventually been able to bring her in, and she could now be clearly heard screaming from the side room, leave me alone. I want to die. I walked in and she was on the floor with two HCA's trying to stop her from repeatedly banging her head on the wall, her stuffed teddy bear by her side covered in blood. I want to die, she screamed, let me die! Has anyone gone to get something to calm her down? I asked, as four of us tried to get her off the floor and onto the trolley so that she didn't harm herself more. She was biting scratching and kicking us as we tried in vain to hold her still, to administer her sedative, thankfully security was there to help, the sedative eventually took hold, and she calmed down, she was curled in a foetal position her teddy bear in her arms, I covered her with a warm blanket, and closed the cubicle curtain, the mental health team would be arriving shortly, to admit her to the psychiatric ward, looking at her sleeping so young and childlike it broke my heart.

I looked around the busy room, all of a sudden, we had an influx of patients, no wonder we were struggling to see them in a timely manner.

Almost on a daily basis on the news, we hear about A&E waiting targets not being met, and hospitals being stretched to breaking point. In fact, it's not just in the emergency room but probably every ward in the entire hospital, if not all hospitals across the country, with people, especially the elderly, waiting for up to Ten hours on a busy hospital corridor to be seen. It is so sad and drives all hospital workers insane, bearing in mind, they are frail, in pain and very scared it's like a scene from a third world country, not one that is supposed to be advanced, not one where people have paid a massive chunk of their hard earned tax into it, it's quite shocking actually, and this problem has gotten to the point of no return over the last decade.

We are so understaffed, nurses are running around trying to juggle about a thousand tasks at once, as well as putting up with abuse and being sworn at, doctors are so few and far between that it's like finding a needle in a haystack when you are looking for one and since GP practices have for some reason stoped seeing patients like they used too, instead telling them to visit the ED, it's no wonder we are not coping, you can see the poor HCAs, the bedrock of any hospital, running around trying to get the bedpans and vomit bowels in place before we become a national health hazard, giving out refreshments and taking observations, everyone is burnt out, young doctors who have already worked their given hours, working overtime to see their patients. Snapping at staff due to their tiredness, then apologising for being rude.

The ever-rising shortage of nursing staff, and care staff is also making it very difficult for us to safely see our patients, and having to resort to agency staff is very costly. But who listens to us mere front-line workers? I'd dread to think what would happen if we ever had a serious pandemic on our hands. I'd dread to think and pray to God that we never do. As I really believe a serious pandemic would stretch us to the point of no return. But I strongly believe our sense of duty and compassion in hard times will enable us to perform miracles, because all health staff work tirelessly to do their best. I hope I am right.

Chapter Eighteen
A Happy Ending

It was a busy Saturday morning, the weather outside grey and miserable. The trauma team had been working around the clock trying to impose some order on the triple pile up the night before—a major RTC, the blur of bodies coming into the department in the early hours, a stream of walking wounded, and bodies too disfigured amongst the blood and debris to seem human. We were all running around like crazy trying to triage patients and help organise some sort of order. There had only been two surgery residents, and the nurses and we had been going for 24 hours straight, the poor nurses taking it, in turn, to work overtime with some breaks in between. I felt exhausted this was my third twelve-hour shift and I felt a little detached from the world. I heard myself answering questions, my eyes felt sore from lack of sleep, going over notes and working on autopilot. I wasn't really there. I could smell my tiredness and the faint mix of perfume and sweat rising from my body, my feet ached from the long hour's standing, the backs of my calves aching. The buzzer went off in bay 12. It was time for Jacks medication. Looking at his notes I noticed that the doctors had prescribed more pain relief. He was brought in a few days ago; he was a quiet patient who didn't complain at all, he was young, and very polite.

"We all took it in turns to make sure he wasn't in pain, the nurses and auxiliaries sitting with him in his darkened room talking to him, as he had no apparent visitors or family.

"His story was particularly heartbreaking, a young man, homeless, sleeping in his car, he didn't have the money to visit a good dentist, and was sadly very unkempt. I woke him gently to give him his medication. He was peacefully sleeping, in a comfortable bed with warm blankets, and was making the most of the short-lived luxury. I was about to hand him the glass of water when something white dropped from his mouth onto his gown. Looking closely, my tired eyes not really registering what I was seeing, I was horrified to see a little maggot it sat there looking at me, it's little white body squirming, I was mortified, and quickly ran out to find the Doctor. We looked into the dark pink cave of his mouth, the little white worms, hidden at the very back of his jaw, his teeth were in dire need of a dentist, he had an awful abscess, making the side of his mouth swell. I watched as the Doctor shone his torch to get a better view, the little critters tried to retreat from the glare of the light, working their way further into the recesses of the man's mouth; slowly, they appeared gone. He turned the light off again, and slowly turned to me. Deme, we seem to have a problem on our hands. The poor sod had a very very rare form of extensive gingival myiasis, this is a very rare disease primarily caused by the infestation of tissue by larvae or horseflies. Oral myiasis like this gentleman had was even rarer, I had never seen anything like this before.

"We couldn't believe what we were seeing. I felt so bad for him. I never thought I'd witness anything as bad as this.

Dr Jacobs laughed at the horrified look on my face and said, "Deme, please, go find me some cotton wool and soak it in turpentine oil." I ran as quickly as I could, grateful for the distraction.

I applied the cotton wool bud with the oil inside his mouth, it worked like magic. The tiny larvae attached themselves to the buds enabling us to grasp them and remove them manually with the help of tweezers, the little bloodsuckers would squirm and wriggle while I would fish them slowly out of his mouth. I did this in half-hourly intervals, dipping the cotton buds soaking them and dabbing them onto the little white squirming bodies, I was patient, and mesmerised working quietly till I had managed to retrieve them all, and his mouth was finally free of the little critters. Over 50 maggots were removed on the first day, one of the most fascinating yet disgusting tasks I have ever witnessed and participated in. On the fifth day of treatment when the infection was controlled, and the wound debrided of all necrotic tissue. The Doctors examined the area of infection in his mouth for any remaining larvae, thank you Deme, Dr Jacob's said, I hope it wasn't to much of a horrendous task for you. He then asked me to get the Max fax team to have a look at him, before the would was sutured with 3-0 silk. He eventually ended up on the Max Fax ward for further treatment and wasn't discharged properly for a further two weeks. I saw the gentleman six months later; he was walking to the max fax department for a routine appointment, it was hard to believe it was the same bloke, he looked like a completely different person, the nurse called his name and he slowly walked to the desk, he was clean shaven, and his brown eyes looked happy, he had clean clothes and looked almost unrecognisable. He also had a complete set of lovely pearly white false teeth, he was a stunning looking young man, I stood there watching him, I couldn't believe the transformation. No one had told him a thing about what was alive in his mouth; he was young and didn't want to look ugly; thankfully, he was blissfully unaware. I found out that he was also no longer living in his car. The Go Fund Me page that the nurses and doctors that day had set up had raised thousands of pounds, so that he was able to buy a small house and he was currently training to be a doctor. He was young and had the drive and determination to make the most of a second chance in life I smiled to myself, thankful that we had made a difference and for once a tragic case had a happy ending.

Chapter Nineteen
The Nightmare Begins

We were in the middle of our third year in practice as newbie trained nurses, no longer trainees; I was now working on the Spinal ward; Phoebe was working in rehabilitation. I had found her leaning against the nurses' station. It was well past midnight, and we were both working the graveyard shift; she looked pale and drawn; her eyes sunken hollows, it also looked like she had lost a ton of weight, the once smiley face gone, in its place, I could see the crow marks of endless worry, her uniform looked creased and stained, she was a shadow of the person I knew before. I was so shocked at her appearance, I asked her what she was doing down in the Spinal ward, and she told me she was down to collect medication for a patient, they were out of stock on her ward, and we are allowed to borrow medication from other wards. I said I'd get her what she needed after I had finished checking on my patient. When I had finished, I went back to her and couldn't help but ask her what was wrong.

"I have been referred," she said, "to the NMC." She whispered carefully so that no one heard her.

"Why?" I said, stunned; she was one of the kindest nurses I knew, not to mention knowledgeable.

"It's a long story; I haven't been able to sleep for weeks."

"Why?"

Looking down at the floor, "I don't want to go into it; she doesn't believe me," by that, she meant the sister who was making the referral, I knew the sister, we all did she was not a nice person vindictive and mean.

She was exhausted with worry. I knew what it was like to be exhausted, dealing with one patient after another, without breaks and short-staffing, the almost military ache in your body as you rush around, running on empty, let alone having the added worry of a referral. I gave her a hug and the medication she had come for, I told her, "My door is always open if you want help, please come round to see me."

I couldn't believe that they had referred her; it had to be every nurse's worst nightmare, you see in order to practise as a nurse, firstly you have to have an up-to-date pin, the second is to not have been referred to the NMC who are the Nursing and Midwifery Council. They are the governing council to whom you pay an annual fee each year to belong to; they make sure that every nurse abides by the rules and regulations set out by the council, even if those rules and regulations are somewhat antiquated. Anybody deemed to not be following them, either have sanctions placed upon their pin, like conditions of practice, are either suspended and therefore not allowed to practice, for a certain amount of time, or worst case scenario they are struck off, which completely fucks up any chances of you ever being able to practice again, well at least for five years. Then they will call you back and make you grovel into saying you have acknowledged your mistake and are a better nurse for this, though why some poor nurse would ever want to humiliate themselves that much is beyond me.

I can understand nurses being struck off for inflicting abuse and theft but getting struck off for something that they didn't even do, or for trivial matters that can be sorted out is downright cruel. The trouble is unless you have evidence that you are innocent and a pocket full of money to hire a good solicitor, you are basically shafted. My advice to any newbie nurse would be to always pay your union fees, as the unions will fight tooth and nail for your cause. In the case of poor Phoebe, she was in so much debt after graduating that all her wages were going back into paying her debtors, so she let her union membership lapse. The irony of this was that she was referred the day after it had lapsed, so she was basically not able to ask them for help. Talk about bad luck.

The rest of my shift went smoothly enough but I couldn't get her out of my mind; I was really worried that she would do something terrible to herself, I was really worried. I made a mental note to go and speak to her before I heard further bad news. After I had gotten some sleep following my shift, I decided to go see her.

Chapter Twenty
Tragedy...

It was past midday before I had woken up following the night shift from hell. I looked at my bedside clock; oh God, I was supposed to go see Phoebe, I promised; I quickly got dressed and ran the two blocks to her apartment. After banging on her door for ten minutes, panic started rising in me. She hadn't messaged me since we last spoke, which was very unusual of her. I was still hammering on her door when her elderly neighbour came out looking worried. "Can I help you?"

"I'm a friend of Phoebe's, and I came to see how she is doing; she works as a nurse in the department next to mine. Have you seen her?"

"No, my dear, I hope she is all right; I have her keys. If it's an emergency, she leaves them with me so that I can let out her little Jack Russell."

I couldn't hear a dog barking or Phoebe; I grabbed her keys and frantically opened the door. The flat was dark; turning on the lights, I saw that it was a tip, rubbish everywhere, pots and pans, laundry on the floor, and dog excrement. I covered my nose, trying not to vomit. I was mortified; this was so very unlike the Phoebe that I knew, the one who was always immaculately turned out. Her flat was a palace, always clean, tidy and smelling of fresh flowers—what was going on for it to look like this? Running around, I frantically called out; it was only then I heard a whimper coming from her bedroom door. I ran towards it, my heart hammering in my chest, my skin had broken out in goosebumps, and I felt sick.

I opened the door, and at first, didn't understand what I was seeing. It was a few minutes before my screams could be heard down the street, and someone must have called the police because I heard the faint sound of the siren. My poor beautiful friend was laying on the floor, a noose round her neck and drying froth from her mouth dripping onto the carpet, her Jack Russell by her side whimpering. I ran to her, praying I'd find a pulse, knowing in my heart of hearts that I wouldn't. The empty medicine bottles lay around her, paracetamol, Tramadol, Morphine. Where the hell did, she get this lot from? Cradling her poor head in my lap, I tried desperately to find a pulse rocking back and forth; my screams and crying could be heard clearly. By that time, the police had arrived along with the paramedics. "Move out of the way, miss," I heard the ambulance technician say, I was trying desperately to give her CPR.

I watched them as they started pummelling her chest, trying to revive her. 20 minutes they continued for. I was numb, standing, watching my dear friend's body lifting each time they tried to resuscitate her. I cradled her Jack Russell in my arms, crying softly into its smooth coat. I then turned round to the police officer, all I could say was, "The bastards have killed her."

I wasn't allowed to collect any of her belongings as it was up to the family to sort that out; also, it would be used as evidence. I gave the police my details and went with the officer to give a statement. Taking her little dog with me as they wanted to put it in a dog sanctuary if nobody claimed her.

The rest of the day was a blur of questions and more questions. I gave my account of how I found her, and the next-door neighbour also spoke to the police. It was 8pm before I managed to get home; opening the door, I found Gianni waiting for me, arms open. Sobbing, I went to him.

The irony of what she went through, and horror fully hit me, when a few weeks later, I read an article in the papers,

"Details of the suicides, which happened in the past year, have been released for the first time by health officials."

Four nurses killed themselves, fearing they would be struck off from working in the NHS.

The move comes amid growing concerns over mental health problems among nurses.

In each case, the health workers were facing Nursing and Midwifery Council (NMC) 'fitness to practise' hearings.

Jennie Hawkins of the Laura Hyde Foundation, set up after a former nurse's suicide, said, "All nurses going through investigation should be offered psychological support to help manage their anxieties and increase their coping skills."

Up until now, it has been very difficult to determine whether nurses had ever harmed or killed themselves while under investigation.

It was only last year the NMC began keeping a record of suicide among nurses during investigations, which can take years to complete.

Last year, the NHS apologised after an independent investigation found a nurse who took his own life after being sacked was treated unfairly.

Reading these awful statistics, I was sickened, and furious and for the first time, I really felt like quitting the profession. *Who needs this shit*, I thought.

Sadly, it would take me another seven years before I plucked up the courage to get out of the profession. Don't get me wrong; I love being a nurse—we all do—I was born to help people, show them compassion and go above and beyond the call of duty to do my best for them. What's changed sadly is this new blame culture, downright nasty nurses and staff shortages, as well as the added fear amongst nurses and doctors in case they are referred to either the GMC, which is the General Medical Council for Doctors, or the dreaded NMC. I hope reading the statistics and lives taken they will start making changes to the way they handle referrals and petty disputes that should have never been referred to in the first place. Sometimes I do wonder if all this is worth it.

For my dear friend and colleague, it's too late; she will never live to see a daughter or son do well; her family will never again hear her infectious laugh. If she had spoken to me, I would have tried my hardest to help her. I never really knew why she was referred; no one had told me. I only found out the shocking truth when I received a letter in the post. Phoebe had written it before taking her life; inside the envelope was a letter outlining the tragic and, in my opinion, illegal way she was treated. The envelope contained her NMC investigation along with a photocopy of the truth as to what had happened.

Reading the contents, I was shocked, angered and above all furious. I really wanted to bring justice to her, even if it was posthumously but I knew this was impossible. My poor dear friend, this should have never happened. My heart will be forever broken for the way a kind-hearted nurse was treated. I only hoped one day that people and Trusts start appreciating and helping nurses in need instead of referring them, and at least offering mental health counselling, and helping them. I know that not all nurses are innocent and there are some horrifically evil and wicked ones. And it's the NMC's job to protect the public. But I also believe far too much time is spent on petty referrals, while the serious cases get overlooked and covered up for prolonged periods of time. What a sad world we sometimes live in. I have worked with some lovely people, nurses and care assistants over the years, many who have become dear friends. But for all the exceptional people in this profession. There are also extremely evil ones, it's surprisingly scary how they manage to get away with the things they do. The news is full of Breaking News stories of Bad evil nurses, and what's shocking is they actually get away with unbelievable things just because they either hide their mistakes well, or are friends with management. Until someone eventually grasses them up. It's a great shame that the good news and great work the majority of doctors and nurses do, goes un reported.

Chapter Twenty-One
People Are Strange

Having worked as a nurse now for nearly eleven years, I have seen many changes to the way we work. But it's not just the work ethic that has changed; people and patients have changed, in fact, I think since social media, the whole world has changed. To say I have seen some pretty bizarre cases come into A&E would be an understatement. There have been too many bizarre cases to mention; however, I will tell the story of one that particularly mortified me.

There was one gentleman who came in who had been injecting drugs intravenously and was known to be HIV positive have contracted the disease from an infected needle. Now having had the dreaded fear of having been infected from my cannula mistake, I felt very sad for the gentleman. But that sympathy would change to downright shock when I found out the true reason for his admission. He came complaining of shortness of breath, which sometimes can be the side effect of the retrovirals that you needed to take to combat the disease; I believed him as I too had the symptoms when I took my PrEP. I took his observations, blood pressure, saturation and temperature; everything came back normal. I couldn't find anything out of the ordinary. I was stumped so called in the doctor; he too agreed with me, everything was as it should be. We had no choice but to refer him for further tests and a stay in the infectious diseases ward, just to be on the safe side. Amazingly enough, he was given expensive drugs for over three days, the nurses believed him when they asked if he had taken his meds. And as no one dared question a patient's integrity in fear of being told off, if they had checked they would have found a bag full of the drugs he was supposed to be taking, he had hidden them carefully. If they had, I dare say, he would have been prosecuted for drug smuggling. What he was doing with these drugs was beyond me, most probably selling them on the street for ridiculous amounts of money, his very own little Dallas buyers club.

This case touched a particularly raw nerve for me; having gone through fear for six months after blood splurged in my eye, I couldn't comprehend why someone would do something like this. But like the *Echo and the Bunnymen* song lyrics say: people are strange!

This case also reminded me of someone who worked in Theatres as an Anaesthetist. Now this brilliant clever bloke wasn't happy with a fairly decent wage. Maybe he got bored, or the lure of more money was too great to resist. Regardless of the reasons, he decided to have a stab at extracurricular drug dealing unbeknown to everyone else. No one knows how he managed to do this, but he was taking small amounts of Midazolam which is a benzodiazepine medication used for anaesthesia and procedural sedation, it is also used to treat severe agitation. However, he was taking small amounts on a daily basis and storing it in the ceiling above the reception area of the department he was working in. He was meticulous and careful. Never thinking he was ever going to get caught.

I heard that by the time the proverbial shit hit the fan for him, he was amassing a cool £3,000 a month extra on top of his NHS wages. This had continued for nearly five years. But like most money hungry people he didn't know when to stop. One day he had come to work and was promptly escorted to the Hospital Directors office. He'd been rumbled. According to the Chinese whispers grapevine. Estates had come in to routinely change one of the ceiling tiles and ironically, the tile they removed was directly next to his Midazolam hiding hole. The only reason they knew it was him was because the idiot had left his diary with his clients contact details with the bag of stash. And the Police decided to ring some of the names in that book and finally one of his clients grassed him up. He managed in five years to make £160,000 not a great deal for a drug dealer but on top of his £30,000 wage packet not bad going. Of course, he lost his licence, was arrested and his marriage broke down he was a disgrace to his family and friends. Maybe he regretted doing what he did. Maybe he regretted getting caught. Now we all have to sign a Drugs book each time we get a delivery. The porters have to sign it when collecting orders; in fact, anyone dealing with any sort of controlled drug has to sign this book otherwise no drugs are given out.

I can't believe the length's people go to to earn an extra buck, and I still occasionally thought about Eva and what she was up to. People can do the strangest things.

Chapter Twenty-Two
Oscar Is on The Prowl

People have always asked me, in my long history in the care profession, if I have ever seen or witnessed things that I have found either strange or couldn't explain. I try to avoid these awkward questions, because to be honest there are so many strange and unexplained events that I have witnessed that it's crazy and would only raise questions about my sanity. People also wouldn't believe me.

Perhaps one of the weirdest things that occurred was when I worked as a bank nurse in a care home. This particular home had a resident black cat named Oscar. The residents loved him, he was a rescue and very old. I loved that cat like he was my own. He was lovely, and during the night shifts when I worked the graveyard shift, he would jump on my lap in the office and keep me company while I was catching up on endless paperwork. Purring away oblivious …so I thought.

Staff who had been there longer than me used to say that Oscar knew when the Grim Reaper was about to make a visit. I didn't believe them of course until I started noticing a strange pattern. You see Oscar would continuously pace up and down outside certain residents' doors. These residents were always on the end-of-life pathway. Maybe that cat could sense this, I don't know but he would prowl outside the bedroom door of the resident, or jump on their bed, sitting purring, staring at them with his black hairs on his back up. It used to freak me out, but I could guarantee that within twenty minutes of doing this they would have peacefully either passed away, or the care assistant would come rushing to the office to get me to check the resident. It happened every time.

I became used to Oscar warning me, and even though it used to freak me out, I would try and make sure that someone was in the room with that resident to comfort them and hold their hand. I hated the thought of the poor old souls dying on their own in fear. Years later I was watching Stephen King's Doctor Sleep, I realised that Oscar was like many Cats, and knew when someone was about to pass away. Just like Azzi in Stephen King's Movie.

Another strange occurrence was when I was working on a ward for the elderly. It was a regular Monday, and I was busy admitting new residents, writing notes and administering medication. At around 11:00, we had a new lady arrive, her name was Mrs Scutt. She was 85 years old and had arrived after having a fall from her care home bed. The injuries were horrific. She had a black eye, terrible swelling to her forehead and a split lip. She was 85 and it broke my heart to see someone so frail suffer so much. She also had advanced vascular dementia.

After we had made her comfortable and given her strong pain relief, she settled down, and appeared to be comfortable. For the remaining of the week we did all we could to offer her dignity, respect and show her compassion. She didn't seem to have any visitors apart from the last few days. Her niece came distraught having to see her in this state. However because she was so highly sedated, she was oblivious to her surroundings and visits. Then something really strange happened. We had a new admission, a lady in her late 70's who didn't speak much English, she was Serbian and was admitted for BM monitoring. She arrived on Thursday, four days later to Mrs Scutt. Neither patient knew who the other was, they were not related and as far as I knew had no reason to interact with each other. Then on Thursday, the most bizarre thing happened. It was teatime and visiting hours. Mrs Scutt's niece had come in to visit. She was sitting at her aunt's side holding her hand. Mrs Scutt was of course unresponsive, she was highly sedated and oblivious to being touched. The lady that had been admitted a few beds down, for no apparent reason got up and walked purposefully towards Mrs Scutt's bed. She then gently sat on her bed and started stroking her hair and cheeks. Now the next thing that happened was unreal.

Mrs Scutt opened her eyes, sat up, as if nothing was wrong and stared at this woman, she then started talking to her, much to the disbelief of her niece, the consultant doing rounds and everyone else. She was lucid and smiling, having a conversation with a total stranger as if she was a dear family member. Her niece was sitting there with her mouth open, unable to speak. Then just like that the patient got up, kissed Mrs Scutt on the forehead and whispered something in her ear, then as if nothing happened walked away and went back to bed. Mrs Scutt then went back into the non-talking oblivious state she was in before this happened.

Because I was busy and had patients to see, I didn't stop to listen to her niece adamantly state that it was her dead grandma that had just visited her aunt. The doctors didn't know what to say because they too witnessed her talking and the lady sitting on the bed. Two days later, Mrs Scutt sadly passed away, and the strange patient discharged herself. This was one of the strangest things I have seen, I can't explain it. Like I say some things are just beyond words and there is no explanation to them. Believe them or disbelieve them, no one can deny that this happened, we all witnessed this strange phenomenon whether we choose to believe it is another matter entirely. A month later, we received a Thank You card from her niece. She had also mentioned that she was grateful to the mysterious lady, and deep down swore that it was her aunt's mother visiting her and offering her comfort before she died.

Chapter Twenty-Three
The Essence of Time

I had just finished a night shift and still wasn't fully recovered from the lack of sleep, so it was no surprise to see me looking haggard. I was in the lift going to the blood bank on the fifth floor of the hospital, when I caught a glimpse of myself in the reflection of the door in the lift. I looked older than I usually do, dark rings under my eyes, the tell-tale signs of a few crows' feet at their corners, I am pale and need my inhaler on a regular basis thanks to my low immune system. Though I could easily pass for a twenty-five-year-old instead of thirty-five. Many of my patients are mildly surprised when they first meet me. Over the years of hard work and struggling I had eventually been promoted to charge sister with my dark blue uniform, the result of hard work, tears and biting my tongue. "Is she really the Sister? Are you sure?" Over the years I had worked my way up tirelessly. The elderly always want to sit and talk to me, you're such a kind nurse one 93-year-old said. I sadly look at them weary, I will always be kind, but my heart is tired, and heavy from everything I have seen, sometimes I have to literally force the smile on my face. having had enough of a decade of heartache, I miss my mother, and think about her daily she should have still been here, if it wasn't for breast Cancer. The staff cuts and austerity measures of the government cuts and more cuts have had a huge impact on the care we try to give. Hospitals and nursing homes are left running on empty. I never fully got over my friend's suicide, and I think of her daily, wondering if I could have done something to help her anything, my heart breaks each time and I feel enraged that our governing body never apologised or was held accountable. The evil sister who had referred her in the first place, still in her job, carries on as if nothing has happened. She was only young-, just starting out in life, I remember her on our first day, all smiles laughing oblivious to what her future held, expectant and proud. Less than four years later, she is dead, never having had the joys of motherhood.

Her family are empty shells, when I visit them to check that they are okay, they look worn out, there once immaculate home gone to disrepair, they make an effort when they see me, asking how I am doing but they don't really care, I can smell the faint odour of whisky under their breaths, the semi slurred words, masking their grief. I never stay long; my heart breaks each time I see them, I don't know how I would cope if the same thing happened to me.

Each day I get up, wear my pressed uniform, and plaster a smile on my face, I hold their hands, my patients the ones I am always there for. In the mornings, I wait for them, they arrive an endless stream of walking wounded, my day is a blur of treating one emergency after another. Some are patient while others are visibly frustrated at having to wait for so long. I move from one patient to the other, ordering urine samples, bloods, listening to their chests, taking their observations. They are angry because they also have to wait, no beds available, we are short staffed. I used to get upset about this, trying my hardest to find beds and make the best of a bad situation. Now their anger has little affect. We are going as quickly as we can, I say please be patient. There are lots of sick people here. More often these days, I am angry. The drug addict who came in with a deep laceration to his head, hair a mass of dark greasy curls his face young and angry, where's my Methadone!

"Hey, I asked for it hours ago," he asks eyes red and bloodshot wild and unseeing. "I have asked the doctor to right you a prescription it's in pharmacy at the moment." Exhausted, I look around the busy department so many patients to see and not enough hours in the day to see them in. I grit my teeth and carry on, six more hours to go, six gone already, my colleagues are all busy running around, smiling fingers deftly stitching people up, making them smile, reassuring the frightened and elderly. My colleagues are the unstoppable, unsung heroes of the general public, angels in disguise.

I look at them, the tired look on their faces, and feel so sorry for them, but also proud that I am a part of them. I am also very sad about the negativity in the press, wondering what it will take for everyone to appreciate them.

I didn't know it at the time of writing this but soon my beloved NHS was going to be tested to the hilt, in the cruellest epidemic outbreak imaginable. But no one knew what was about to happen. And the devastating effect a new epidemic that nobody understood was going to have on not only the UK but the world over.

Chapter Twenty-Four
Outbreak

Every year for as long as I have been nursing, which amounts to quite a while, we have had a contagious disease outbreak crisis of one form or another. It's either a superbug gone rampant, like the NoroVirus which symptoms at its worst includes a very high temperature of over 42 degrees, a hacking cough that doesn't seem to end and it's residue can last for up to six months, vomiting till your stomachs doesn't have anything left in it, add onto this a Recurrent Urinary Tract Infection, in layman's terms a UTI and you wish you were dead already. I have only had the Norovirus once in my life, I am a fairly healthy individual that exercises and eats the right food, and follows all the health and safety measures, put in place to avoid contracting diseases especially in my line of work. Yet I still managed to be infected, and to make matters worse this happened during the Christmas Holidays. Thankfully, I isolated myself to avoid others contracting it, especially the elderly and vulnerable, it was quite an outbreak, with whole wards closing off and extra measures put into place and it was horrific, I had a temperature of 39 plus was vomiting every hour as well as having Diarrhoea and to make matters worse, I couldn't stop coughing. On average thousands of elderly and those with underlying health issues suffer the most each year mainly resulting in death, epidemics and outbreaks like the NoroVirus, Ebola & D&V, impact seriously on NHS resources and kill thousands but the amazing doctors, nurses and health workers up and down the country they all pull-together and tirelessly work to save lives and do their best during times of great stress and challenging circumstances. I think that every single Nurse and Health professional I have had the honour are angels in disguise and I feel very privilege to work with. Even though we have faced austerity cuts, bureaucracy and staff shortages. We always do our very best to save people, we treat them with respect, dignity and above all compassion.

However, a new virus had come to town and if we thought we could handle it like we did the others over the years, we were in for a huge surprise. Covid 19 was about to raise its ugly head and hit not only the public but the NHS in the most devastating fashion that would test everyone, our freedom, partying, and our health and humanity as we know it was about to change forever. My life was definitely about to change in ways I could never have imagined, not in my wildest dreams or worst nightmares.

Chapter Twenty-Five
28 Days Later

The year had started well for me, I had recently started a new job. I had had enough of A&E and needed a break. So I applied for a job in Theatres specialising in endoscopy procedures, and even though my boss was a cantankerous, bad tempered and sarcastic individual I still enjoyed my job. It had been a hard year for us all working in the NHS, and the care profession as a whole, Covid 19 had taken a lot of lives in the front line, colleagues who had dedicated all their working lives caring for others, where themselves ending up in ICU fighting for their life. Young nurses and doctors, and care workers, where dropping like flies. It was a scary time, and everyone was at their wits end, we didn't know what to do for the best. Also to add insult to injury we were running low on PPE, and in extreme cases, had to resort to wearing out of date protective clothing, I guess any clothing was better than none at all, but I still thought, how bizarre and downright illegal is that. I wondered who was actually profiting from providing this to the NHS. Okay so the general public were clapping for us, which was great, but clapping wasn't helping the staff shortages, the long hours with hardly any breaks, not to mention the high rise in sick leave and general burnout trying to save people. It also wasn't helping the low morale we were all feeling, nurses and care workers ending up in tears, with the crazy working conditions, and PPE equipment, that made you feel like you were suffocating, unable to breathe standing caring for your patients for 14 hours with hardly any breaks. To add further insult to injury, we were not even allowed to hug them to make them feel better. I counted myself lucky not to have been hit by Corona. I thought that because I was being very cautious, following all the social distancing and mask wearing guidelines, hand washing regularly and being very vigilant and careful that I had a good chance of dodging it for a little longer.

I was worried about Covid, like we all were but because I had managed to test negative for nearly a year, I felt like one of the lucky ones. So, each week on a Tuesday, I tested myself at work using the test kits provided, and luckily enough it came back negative. On Wednesday the 20th of January 2021, I was running late for work, I was panicking and didn't want to let my team down, so I ordered a taxi. I was extra vigilant and even wore latex gloves in the cab so as not to have to touch anything. The cab driver however was not wearing a mask. I arrived at work within minutes of having to start my shift, I was feeling a little bunged up and the back of my neck was aching but other than that, I had no temperature, and wasn't coughing. I was on my break and decided to go take my Covid test. To my surprise, it was again a negative result but I thought I had no cough or temperature and had my taste and smell. I can't possibly have Covid. I thought that I was coming down with the flu, so that night I had a warm bath, took two paracetamol and went to bed a little earlier than usual. The next morning, I felt a little better. This was a

Thursday, and it was my half day at work, I had Friday off and all the weekend to recoup and recharge my batteries. To be honest over the weekend other than an achy neck and muscles I felt fine, I had the occasional sneezing fit but again I thought nothing of it, as I suffer from hay-fever and allergies anyway and even though it was winter, I still suffered from hay-fever-like symptoms. On Monday, I went back to work as again I had no obvious Covid symptoms, again no fever or cough. I told myself I have my test again tomorrow and hopefully it will put my unease to rest, I didn't really worry about having Covid. On Wednesday the 27th of January my life as I knew it changed forever, you guessed it, my Covid test came back positive. My boss came to me with my results and told me to go home. I was escorted out of the building so that I wouldn't touch anything, bloody hell I thought this was scary. I honestly felt mortified and like a leper. I could see other staff members whispering and pointing in my direction. I honestly felt like I had committed murder. When I arrived home, I had too immediately self-isolate. I didn't want Gianni catching this, so I traced my steps and wiped everything down with my Dettol antibacterial wipes and went immediately to bed. I felt like death.

When I woke up, it was Friday. I'd lost three days. I had slept for nearly 74 hours and instead of feeling better, I was getting gradually worse. I literally didn't have the energy to move. My muscles ached, I felt so weak I could hardly move, and I also had a terrible stomach ache and desperately needed to go to the toilet. I was so weak and disoriented by that time, that I didn't make it in time to the toilet. I have never been so embarrassed in all my life. I tried my hardest to clean up my mess as I didn't want Gianni to have to see me in this way.

The poor bloke was sleeping in the spare room, but I was so weak that I collapsed with a loud thud on the bedroom floor. The racket must have been heard downstairs because he came rushing upstairs. I was in bed struggling to breath. He took one look at me and called the paramedics. I started crying as I didn't want to go into hospital, and I certainly didn't want anyone to see me in this god-awful mess, with diarrhoea and vomit all over me. I needed to clean up and have a shower, so I literally dragged myself to the shower and with the willpower of a mad woman, I just about managed to wash the excrement off my body and vomit out of my hair but for the love of money, I didn't have the energy to dry my hair. I dragged my weak body out of the bathroom, and just about managed to make it back to my bedroom and pass out in bed…

I woke up to two paramedics standing at the bottom of the bed staring at me, one started getting an ECG monitor out, the other was taking my temperature and telling me to take the covers off me and open the bedroom window as I had a temperature of 40. I was given two paracetamols but because my Oxygen saturation was 90% they told me to keep an eye on my symptoms and ring another ambulance, if I felt any worse, they then quickly left. I think they didn't want to be in the same room with me and I don't blame them, even though they were wearing masks I was extremely ill and highly contagious. The time was 6pm. I fell back into a deep but fitful sleep. Gianni came back to check on me at around 8:30 pm. My lips were blue, and I couldn't breathe well at all. I was starting to get a little scared, because all I could hear in the distance was a lot of shouting and someone crying on the phone telling whoever to hurry up, she's not well. I think she is dying. After that, I must have passed out completely.

I woke up on the set of E.T the extra-terrestrial, a man in a boiler suit and breathing apparatus was standing over me on a walkie talkie, telling whoever was on the other end to bring the gurney up and make it fast.

"What's wrong?" I said. "What's going on? Where is ET?"

This soothing voice said, "It's okay, my dear; we are just checking you over. Your saturations are extremely low in the 70's and you need to go to hospital immediately."

"I'm not going anywhere E.T needs me." I kept on jabbering talking complete nonsense all the while that I was being strapped to the gurney, with an oxygen mask on me. When the mask was in place, I felt this wonderful sensation of air, and took a gulp full of O2. I felt like I was in heaven. My lungs took in that air like my life depended on it, and of course it did because by that time, I was showing signs of hypoxia and delirium. The guy from the E.T set was outside rushing to the side of the ambulance, while two other guys in the same space suits were carrying me as quickly as they could to the ambulance. I looked around, strange that so many neighbours are out. I wonder if they are looking for E.T too. A sharp scratch jolts me out of my daydream.

"Ouch, what the hell?"

"Sorry but we need to take your blood. Don't worry you are in safe hands, just relax and keep taking deep breaths." What I saw next was really weird and other than mentioning it to you the reader of this book I haven't mentioned it to anyone; they would think I was completely stark raving mad. I felt like the ambulance was full of people, but people don't have wings and lights around them. I tried to think rationally, am I finally losing my mind. *Where am I going*? Fear started to grip me, and of course with the fear my heart rate started rising. I was so upset that it rose to almost 120 bpm. By that time, my saturations were slowly rising to 83%. But my blood pressure was rather low 95/60, very low indeed even for me. The voices were getting louder sounding more urgent. There is a bed on Fleming Ward, I heard one paramedic say, and with that, the blue light went on and off I went to hospital, my breathing laboured even though I was on full oxygen.

"Keep taking deep breaths, sweetheart," a kind voice kept saying, stay with us "we will be there as soon as possible."

I don't remember much after that, only the sounds of people around me, doctors and nurses a blur of blue scrubs. I remember being placed on a ventilator and having my observations taken. I also remember a cannula being placed in my arm and being attached to a bag of liquid. Bloods and injections continued throughout the night. I just about managed to get some sleep, when another nurse came up to me to give me medication and encourage me to drink water. My blood pressure was still very low.

I was desperate to go to the toilet, and drinking all the water I was offered didn't help. I was very weak and could hardly get up. Thankfully, a really kind student nurse named Megan helped me get up and held my hand while I hobbled to the toilet. It was such a relief. Shaking, I grabbed onto the washbasin to drag myself up. It was only then that I managed to look at myself in the mirror. I couldn't believe it. My eyes were sunken black holes. My lips looked cracked and dry. I was almost translucent, and my skin had a weird yellow tinge to it. My hair was matted, mangled and stood on end. *Wow, I could easily pass for Reagan in the Exorcist,* I thought. Dizziness overtook me, and I could hear a loud bell going off outside.

I don't recall getting back to my bed after that. In fact, I don't recall much, other than nurses and doctors rushing around me, ventilators hissing, and my painful laboured breathing trying to get enough oxygen into my lungs to stop me dying.

The doctors and nurses on Fleming Ward must have worked nonstop to keep me alive, apparently because of my delirium and altered mental state brought on by hypoxia I had tried to tie the red emergency cord round my neck. They had frantically tried to open the bathroom door and managed to remove it in the nick of time. I remember having an infusion with this new trial drug, which I should have consented to but due to my poor health and delirium was unable to do this. So, they went ahead with it anyway. Am I angry that they did this, I don't really know, all I know is that I'm alive due to whatever alchemy they induced me with. Would I sue them like some are trying to do, most definitely not, what the general public fail to understand is that doctors and nurses are trying their best to save their patient's life, nobody wants a dead patient. I have seen doctors, nurses and consultants break down in tears when someone has died. It goes against the hippocratic oath to not do their very best for the patient, and I suppose this new drug was what they thought was best. I was slowly but gradually understanding what was going on around me, as my delirium was abating, and I was slowly and gradually returning to the land of the living. I was on a ventilator for three weeks; on the fourth week they started weaning me off it and placed me on a nasal oxygen.

I was still very weak but was more aware of what was going on around me. The ward was rammed with patients. I could see Military personnel wheeling beds in and out of the ward. This really scared me. *My God this has to be bad,* I thought, *who gets the Army in if it's not serious.* I remembered I watched a film called Contagion about three years prior to Covid but it was very uncanny how accurate and true to Covid this film was. I do sometimes wonder if this was an experiment gone wrong, I watched in horror as daily one patient after the other was quietly wheeled into the private room, I realised after a while that the private room was where they went before they sadly passed away. This terrified me, I didn't want to die, the doctors treating me did everything, I remember one constant donned in the horrible PPE equipment with tears in his eyes, the constant patient mortality around him, causing him severe distress, I remember himholding my hand and saying, come on Deme you can do it, you can pull through.

Slowly but surely, I was getting better, I was still very weak, and could only take small steps to the toilet. My legs didn't feel like my own, they felt like lead, and they hurt so much. By the end of the fourth week, I was allowed to go home. By this time, I had started eating a little, but I still looked gaunt. My legs and energy were dire, and I could only manage very small walks back and forth to the ward toilet. Prior to being discharged, I weighed myself, and was shocked to find that I had lost a stone and a half.

On the day of my discharge, I rang Gianni to collect me from the entrance to the ward. I had no medication to collect therefore I didn't need to wait for Pharmacy to dispense the drugs. When Gianni collected me, he was shocked to see my weight loss. He also seemed very quiet and oddly withdrawn.

I was so weak that I didn't really pay much attention to his attitude. I put it down to worrying about me and working long hours. I slowly but surely started getting my energy back but was still off work. It was around two and a half months after I had been discharged that I noticed something really strange.

I had always had beautiful long hair that was my pride and joy, I don't know when I started noticing the difference in its thickness but on this particular day after having a shower, I sat down to comb and blow dry my hair. I started combing it and to my shock and horror, noticed more hair than usual in my brush. I thought at the time that this was probably normal due to the health stress I had just gone through but thought that I'd keep an eye on it. The next day, I combed it again, and this time yet more hair kept coming out. This freaked me out so much I ran upstairs to the bedroom and for some reason looked at my pillow. Why I hadn't noticed this before I don't know but big clumps of hair were on my side of the bed, on the floor and literally everywhere. I froze. I looked in the mirror and could clearly see that the top part of my hairline looked thinner than it usually did with big bold patches. What the hell was going on, I thought. I am slowly getting over nearly dying for my hair to now start falling out.

I rang and grabbed my mobile to ring the doctors. I needed to find out what was going on. I also messaged Gianni to see how he was but got no reply back. My doctors couldn't fit me in for at least a fortnight. So I did what I told thousands of patients not to do. I looked up hair loss and Covid on Google. What it came up with was a condition called Telogen

Effluvium. It's a natural process in the hair cycle of growth. And if someone suffers from either severe stress or illness, this can cause the hair to go into the resting stage of growth. Basically in layman's terms, Telogen effluvium is the name for a common cause of temporary hair loss due to the excessive shedding of resting or Telogen hair after severe illness. The hair usually stops shedding after 100 days. However, looking at the sorry state of affairs my hair was in I was certainly not going to wait for it to reverse itself.

I booked myself the first possible hairdressers appointment that I could find and had what hair was left chopped into a short pixie cut.

Miraculously as soon as I did that, I noticed a few weeks later that it had appeared that my hair had started to slowly stop falling out, what bloody irony. Covid not only had an effect on my strength and breathing but also in my mental well-being. I felt so depressed and low most of the time. I was crying all the time, still felt weak, and couldn't get my words out. I needed a break. I was at just about breaking point.

My boss in the theatre was being impatient with me and was asking when I was going back to work and as I was still on probation, I couldn't have too much time off. So, I bit the bullet and even though I felt like death, I knew that I had to go back to work.

Eight months later, I am slowly getting my stamina back, I am still tired and don't have energy most days and suffer from excruciating Osteoarthritis, but I carry on. I won't give up. How can I give up a decade of caring, seeing friends and colleagues plod on.

I am proud to say I served as a nurse for a decade and will look back on my experience with pride and Joy but since

Covid, its effect on my health, the NHS and the UK in general I have just about had enough. Keep Calm and Carry on, they say...

I love my job, but it is becoming very stressful. If we were short staffed before and buckled under pressure, the effect Covid has had, has been even more devastating. Staff are now leaving the NHS at a more alarming rate than before, and sick absence has tripled. Save our NHS they say we are all scared, fed up and all the promises the government have made have sadly come too late for too many.

I'm not a gambler and I don't know what made me even contemplated going to a Casino but I thought if Boris locks the country down again this would be my last chance to enjoy a night out. So I bit the bullet and thought why not.

Chapter Twenty-Six
Lucky

"What are the odds?" I asked Gianni the question, two minutes after he had walked through the door, he didn't even have time to kiss me, not that he did that a lot these days.

"What are you talking about, *agape mou*?" winning, I said. I was so engrossed with this thought, that I didn't even notice him staring at me, like I'd completely lost the plot.

"Sweetness, have you had any rest today? You are aware that you are due to work another twelve-hour night shift, in approximately half an hour. Darling, I know it's hard for you especially being tired all the time and having long Covid symptoms, I can fully accept crazy talk from you, tiredness does that to you."

"I can assure you it's not crazy talk, I'm serious! I have had enough, this profession is draining us all especially me, do you know that the other day while I was out buying groceries, I was passing the food bank and I was mortified to see Sandra in there queuing with her young daughter, she would have died of humiliation if she had seen me."

"What sort of sick shit is that? A nurse resorting to food banks? Yes, sweetheart, we all have had enough, and we all know the NHS is on its knees but unless we win the lottery our situation is never going to change."

"Oh can't you see that I'm tired and constantly drained and have no energy since bloody Covid! Can't you understand? Oh never mind."

I walked off too pissed off for words he didn't understand at all. "Let me fix you something to eat," he shouted after me, "then I can drop you off at the hospital, or else you are going to be late."

"I'm not going in." I could hear him now getting angry but then he wasn't himself since I had come out of hospital. "Hon, who is going to pay the bills?" He said, his voice rising. "Have you completely lost your mind?"

"No, I have finally woken up! I'm going to change the course of our future forever and if you don't want to join me the door is there. I have rung in sick and I'm already due a holiday, so I have requested my annual leave. I know it's not going to do me any favours, especially at work but I have a hunch that something big is going to happen. Now if you want to know what I have in mind, meet me at the Casino at ten pm, I'll be at the roulette table, don't be late." I finished applying my make-up and gave my little black dress a once over it hung just right especially after my Covid weight loss, I had lost in the region of three stone, had spent a month in ICU and still wasn't fully recovered, but I had a strange tingling feeling, a feeling that was like a gut instinct, I never used to believe or pay much attention to these feelings, but for once I decided to listen to that inner voice. The Manolo's on my feet were already aching me so I grabbed my ballet pumps and rammed them in my bag just in case, I had a feeling it was going to be a long night.

The taxi was waiting for me outside. "Bye, honey I shouted to Gianni," Silence, I slammed the door and ran down the porch steps. "To the Athena Casino please." The driver started the metre running. I sat back wearing sterile gloves, a mask and all the relevant PPE I could muster without looking ridiculous. I did not want to get Covid again. Little did I realise sitting in the back of that car how my life as I knew it was about to change forever.

The Casino was packed for a Thursday night, the air heavy with perfume and eager anticipation, young twenty-somethings on a night out—students having fun, not a care in the world. Enjoying the Christmas restrictions freedom. Some wore masks, others did not. Mine was going to stay firmly in place.

I looked around me, middle aged men who reminded me of my dad, obviously rich beyond belief stood there placing bets, on their arms their blonde voluptuous arm candy firmly attached to their hips, perfectly coiffured, smelling of Chanel, expensive jewellery gleaming in the lights, their makeup professionally applied with long nails like talons.

All these women and men standing at the table placing their bets, on a weeknight, it was a totally different world from the one I was used to, the constant flow of blood, and abuse, breaking bad news, and paperwork, how the other half lived I thought looking around me with envy. Some of them were novices like me, others hard pros probably with a lot of tricks up their sleeves. I had googled how to play roulette for a while, I'd say nearly a year and liked to think that I wasn't a complete novice. But I didn't hold out onto the thought that I'd ever win not in a million years.

I went to the desk to collect my chips. The cashier, a bored looking twenty-something, raised her eyebrows when I placed the two thousand on the counter. Feeling lucky she purred, again she was another immaculate dressed brunette with long perfect looking hair, and make up. I felt self-conscious. Here I was dressed in my simple black dress, I looked tired and definitely not immaculate as I had done nearly a 45-hour week already. I looked at her and said maybe I am. I had spent months training going over my moves and getting to know all the rules, the ins and outs of Roulette, was I a pro? Hell no but I was going to give it and my two grand my best shot. Let's get this straight I'm not stupid nor a gambler and I knew that my chances of winning were remote unless I had a stroke of pure luck.

I felt that even though my luck in the real world was running out faster than it was coming in, I felt like I had nothing to lose and surely after the last few months, It was about time I had some good luck. I had a gut feeling that Lady Luck was on my side tonight I don't know why I felt that way, but I just did, if I had listened to my gut feelings throughout my life things would have perhaps turned out differently for me, but I never did, so for once I thought I'd listen, to that inner voice, I had nearly died from Covid, what more could go wrong? I also still had thirty thousand saved in the bank, so even if everything went pear shaped tonight, I knew I had enough to start over.

I stood there ready to place my bet. "Number 7," I said nervously watching the croupier place my chips on the table, the chips gleamed and the crowd fell silent. Lucky number 7, my day and month of my birthday, the month I qualified, the date of the day I first met Gianni, all the wonderful things that

I gave blessings for, all on one little number 7, they say the number seven is a sign of good luck, I hoped for once the superstitions were real.

The wheel went round and round. With each spin, my heart began beating faster and faster, I felt faint like I did on my first day watching the instructor performing that autopsy, when I had to watch him cut her skull open, only this time I was in a packed casino and there was no exit for me to escape to for fresh air. That funnily enough was when I first fully got to meet Gianni, and first fell in love, though neither of us knew what was going to happen back then. We could have never predicted what was going to happen a few years later. I mean look at tonight still no reply from him. I looked around the room, it was past ten and yet he hadn't arrived.

God, he must be so very pissed off at me; my heart sank. Was I about to lose everything? Gianni, two grand my reputation, everything was on the line. Round and round, the chip went, my life flashed past me with it. The last 19 years of joy and heartache, leaving Greece, my mother's death, struggling through Nursing school, being sick and depressed, sacrificing everything for my health and sanity to do the job I once loved.

What did it all amount to? Was it really worth it? All the staff I had met, the friendships gained. The shock of my best friend's suicide still haunted me to this day. The tears and laughter we shared; the patients we helped save. I'll never forget the look of pure joy on a colleague's face when she found out she was pregnant. Staff had put a fund together to help her pay for a second round of IVF treatment following a heart-breaking failed attempt, and to everyone's pure joy this time it had worked. Care staff are full of heart and compassion, well the good ones are anyway.

Round and round the chips go, where they stop no one knows, silence. I closed my eyes fighting back the tears, holding back the panic, my fingers were tingling, I could feel the start of a major panic attack. The room was deathly quiet, just the click, click, of the roulette table. I couldn't breathe, my mouth was dry, and I began to cough. Then the uproar! Screaming, shouting, clapping I slowly opened my eyes.

"What was going on?" I was so lost in thought, and fear that I had disappeared into a world of my own, the screaming had brought me back to reality.

"Oh my honey …you won." The blonde arm candy was hugging me screaming in my ear, congratulating me like I was her best buddy. Champagne was being brought to me by the bucket loads, by total strangers. Later on when I had finished accepting drinks and envious well wishes, I took my chips to the counter, to collect my winnings. I knew from the screams and champagne that I had done well but not exactly how much I had won.

The same brunette was at the counter. This time, she had a ten-watt smile across her face, and the sarcasm was gone. "Well, well, well," she said with what sounded like respect or it could have been envy. "I have heard of beginner's luck but never this amount of luck. You do understand that it will have to be a check. Do you have any ID?" Luckily, I had my passport and driver's licence in my purse along with a bank statement, and my nurse's name badge a bag full of junk. As she finished writing the check, she had to call the casino manager. "Everyone gets involved. She said, especially with amounts like this." Finally, after half an hour of signing countersigning and security checks, I was allowed to leave with my check. "We have ordered you a taxi just in case, imagine getting mugged with that amount on you, well we hope to see you again soon miss, congratulations once again."

The night air was charged with an electric energy, the stars shone brightly, and the air felt milder, crazy as it was winter. I wrapped my coat and scarf around me tightly. I needed the fresh air.

Instead of getting into the taxi ordered, I decided to walk. I am now quite scared of getting into Taxis considering the risks of Covid. Walking was risky I know with the huge check in my bag but nobody was around at this time. After all, it was two am on a working week night, who in their right mind would be. It was a ten min walk back to the campus and I was way too charged up to sit still. As I neared the neighbourhood, I passed a homeless person, looking closely I could tell she was awake.

"Hello," I said, bending down so that I didn't intimidate her. "Do you not have anywhere to go tonight, a shelter that can put you up? It's so dangerous being out here on your own, especially with the rowdy drunks leaving the clubs, and you look worn out."

She looked at me through sad eyes; she must have been about my age, with big beautiful blue eyes and stunning eyelashes. She was very petite, almost waif-like, holding a bag that had seen better days, close to her chest, rocking back and forth. I looked close at her, something shiny caught the light, as I looked closely I could make out a name tag, Joy in cursive letters. I looked at her again, her name and those eyes rang alarm bells in my head. Joy, where the hell did I recognise that name? Come to think of it, where did I recognise the bag? I knew I had seen it before but for the life of me I couldn't place where.

The girl started talking. "I'm not a freak you know, please stop staring at me, go away and let me sleep." I felt really bad, I know I must have been staring at her, and I hadn't even given her any money. I took my purse out of my bag, careful not to drop the check, and apologetically took out two fifty pound notes, the only thing left in my purse.

"Please don't spend this on drugs, get something to eat and a place to sleep tonight."

She looked at me in disgust, I'm not a drug addict you know! I felt so bad. I was technically rich and here was this poor girl with nothing. I wished I could give her more but at that time I just didn't have any more cash on me, and my bank card was at home. "Well take care and please be safe, use that money for food, please."

"What the fuck do you care what I do with it, if you want the money back, take the fucker, but if not piss off and let me sleep." With a heavy heart, I apologised and started walking the last few yards home. As I ran up the steps and turned the key in the door, it hit me. Joy, my university friend? What the hell, oh sweet Jesus the realisation hit me like a punch in the guts.

"Gianni, I screamed Gianni!" running into our bedroom. Foolishly thinking he was going to be there. The room was empty other than an envelope with my name on it.

My heart broke—Gianni, the love of my life, my soulmate was gone. I nervously opened the envelope.

My darling girl,

Things have changed between us. I can't say how or why, I have no excuse for what I have done. But I owe you the truth, I'm afraid I have been seeing Eva a fellow consultant for the past few months, and even though I feel ashamed of myself. I am afraid that I'm in love with her, we are moving in together, I'm so sorry but it's over between us. Please don't be upset. I will always remember our wonderful time together. I hope you had fun last night and won a few hundred pounds. Maybe you can treat yourself.

All my love,
G.

I didn't know what to say, the prick of all the lousy, evil, nasty things to do to someone, this was pure callousness. The fuck how the hell did I not see this coming. I ran to the wardrobe and found his clothes gone. I sat sobbing unable to believe that this was happening. Finally I got up and went to the kitchen, opened the fridge and took out the champagne that was supposed to be for us both, and drank the contents completely forgetting my check in my bag I then promptly passed out.

Chapter Twenty-Seven
Quitting for New Beginnings

The next morning after I finally woke up, I realised that last night something big had happened but I couldn't remember what exactly. Looking around the room, I found my bag and emptied it on the bed. There was a check from the Casino in there for £75,000. Oh my God. Then everything came rushing back to me. I felt sick, I couldn't breathe but I also felt relieved, the win meant that along with my inheritance I could potentially start over, even leave and go abroad to live. I also remembered that Gianni was gone, the asshole had left without so much as a goodbye, the spineless snake, that's how much he gave a shit about me something about being with Eva, and an affair that had been going on for months, how did I not see that coming, I should have realised something was going on that day he was so upset at her departure. Bonny came trotting towards me tail wagging. "Come here honey, you poor doggy, don't worry, princess, I sat holding her crying, realising that Gianni never really cared about me. I stroked Bonny and whispered in her fur; you will never be left on your own for long hours again little one I promise."

The check sat on the table between me and my fourth mug of coffee. I couldn't bring myself to touch it, in case it was all a dream and at any given moment, I would wake up and smell the reality of being two grand worst off and this was just some sick joke. Boyfriend less and depressed but no – it was real enough my name was written clearly with the five digit number clearly written and signed by the casino. I was rich. Actually, I was rich enough to start a new life.

I quickly got dressed, I was shaking my heart pounding. *I need to go put this in the bank, ASAP, before I either lost it or it was stolen.* Sitting in the bank manager's office trembling slightly, I filled in the forms for a new bank account and sat in silence as the manager explained how I could withdraw the money once it had cleared, did I need a financial adviser, no I replied, I knew exactly what I was going to do.

On the way home as I was planning what to do, especially now that I was newly single. I again passed Joy, this time she had Mac Donald's wrappers all around her and a big steaming mug of coffee. I smiled at her again this time instead of being rude. She got up and hugged me. "Please let me apologise for the way I spoke to you this morning. Thank you so much for the money. I was so very hungry."

"Joy is that you?"

I stared at her closely and then she lowered her eyes in shame and embarrassment. Joy, the kind neuroscience nurse? "It's not you, is it, surely not! How could I forget, you're the nurse who was given such a bad time because you were too honest."

"Bad time." She laughed bitterly. "I lost everything!" Tears were starting to well up in her eyes. "They ruined me."

She was becoming hysterical and people were starting to stare.

"I looked at her, my heart broke she was so young and looked so sad instinctively knew I had to do something to help her, my heart broke thinking about the way she was treated. I sat down next to her, grab your things, Joy, you're coming home with me we will find a solution you can't stay here. This was a spur of the moment thought but hell, I had to do something, I couldn't let her be homeless, I would be mortified if I was in her position after all my hard work and training."

When Joy had finished taking a very long bath, I made her breakfast and gave her fresh new clothes.

She looked like a totally different person; she was extremely thin and looked ill. While she was bathing, I had decided I wanted to help her out. Writing a check for £120,000 enough for her to start over, I placed it in an envelope for when she had rested. She was so tired that when she went to sit down in the lounge she immediately fell into a deep sleep.

When she was fully rested, I sat down to break what I hoped was going to be good news. Opening the envelope, she looked confused. "What's this?" she asked. I spoke before she had a chance to ask any more questions.

"Joy, I want to help you, no one should go through what you have. It's a disgrace and inhumane. This should help you get back on track and start a new career. You have always loved art and writing; this can help you start over. But I have no fixed abode or bank account. I have spoken to the estate agent and have told them that you will be staying in this house temporarily, the £120,000 should be enough to secure a mortgage when you find the right place. It will be a decent enough deposit. You can use the rest to train and still have enough to live on and pay a three-year mortgage in advance. Do something that makes you happy. Forget the bad past, I want to help you and won't accept no for a answer. It's time you had a break try and look to the beautiful future you deserve it, don't let the bastards win, she was so shocked she couldn't answer, I felt so happy that I was able to help her, god knows what I would have done if I was in her position, the poor girl, I thanked the lucky stars that I was in the position to do something, while she slept I started scrolling the internet for properties for sale both in England and abroad."

Chapter Twenty-Eight
C'est La Vie

The small village of Pedino sparkled like a diamond, on the Taygetos Mountains of the southern peninsula of the Peloponnese. Sprawling down from the mountains to the nearby beach, the village consisted of beautiful pale stone Mani Towers and old ochre houses with blue, white and lime green shutters, flowers bloomed everywhere the scent of Jasmine was heavy in the air, gazing out to the sparkling sea, surrounded by pine trees and shrubs my new life awaited me.

We had travelled for nearly five days, taking it in turns, across Europe, Bonny Phoebe's Jack Russell in the back seat sleeping most of the way. I had adopted her soon after the funeral. It was Phoebe's wish that she went to a good home. After the win and a long, long talk with Joy I had decided to start afresh. I had had enough of the day-to-day hardship of working on the front line, weary and disillusioned with false promises from the government, promising change and more staff, along with the terrible viral outbreaks and pandemics. After fifteen years of working the front line, I needed a change. As I came from Greece I decided after a long debate to go back home. I had always wanted to open an animal sanctuary, and having seen the number of strays in Greece knew that this was something I wanted to do. Joy loved writing and needed a break from the streets. I never did ask how she lost everything, I felt bad enough for her as it was. I had heard rumours that she had been referred to the NMC and they were making her life a misery. I was so glad I had given all that up, I loved nursing but hell it wasn't worth committing suicide over or becoming homeless.

Winning seventy-five thousand plus the 1m inheritance I had received when my mother passed away, I had a total of four hundred and twenty-five thousand pounds, enough if I was careful to last me a few years.

I eventually chose the beautiful peninsula of the Peloponnese down the southern side of Greece's mainland.

I was initially considering going to live in Thessaloniki but decided that the beautiful laid back life and astounding beauty of the Peloponnese was too great to resist.

The house that I wanted to purchase was being sold by a British couple wishing to move back to England. They had had a terrible time, I heard from the neighbours, that when they first arrived, they had been involved in an accident and ended up being treated for months at the local hospital with broken limbs. They had a young child and found that they were struggling, the mother having constant flashbacks of the accident. They had a beautiful stone-built Mani Tower, with an abundance of land, and a swimming pool. I had contacted them on eBay after they had advertised their property on the site. The best thing about the property was not only its immaculate condition and stunning views but the price. The poor couple was so desperate to sell that they were willing to lose hundreds of thousands of pounds and were selling it for the bargain price of 65,000 euros, which was about £75,000.

Which left me with enough money to start over. I kept my promise and gave Joy the £100,000 to help her get off the streets, I couldn't let her suffer, I needed to do something, she wouldn't accept the money at first, but I eventually pursued her to take it. After all it wasn't really my money, I had won it. I contacted the young couple immediately and placed a bid of £80,000 an extra five thousand on top of the asking price. The young girl cried tears of gratitude over the phone, thanking me so much. She also informed us that it was fully furnished as they couldn't bring their furniture back. The extra five thousand would enable them to start again in England.

I thanked her and asked her to send her bank details to me via an email, as I didn't want her to pay the extortionate eBay selling fees. So, the best way to do it was to take the property off eBay and do a private sale with a solicitor. I had a good friend in Athens who knew people that wouldn't rip off the poor couple.

Everything was estimated to be done and signed for within 20 weeks especially with the way things were as far as Covid was concerned, longer than both of us had anticipated. But looking at the time line, this would take us into April-May, a beautiful time of year in Greece.

It was a busy time for both me and Joy packing things, organising the freight for our belongings. and me quitting my job. We both enjoyed a quiet peaceful Christmas not doing a great deal at all. Joy spent most of the time in bed catching up on needed sleep. I thought she deserved it. Gianni sent me a Christmas card asking to stay in touch. *Fuck you*, I thought.

Hope you have a great life with Eva, you deserve each other, I thought to myself, if he caught a whiff of the fact, I was now semi rich, he might try and worm his way back. *Bollocks*, I thought, *serves you right*. I was still fuming, I knew something was going on between him and Eva, but I was so blindsided by by his charms that I didn't act on my suspicions. But Karma has a wonderful way of working out when you least expect her to.

It took a total of five months for everything to be completed. I was so ready for my new life, looking at Bonny as she wrapped her little body on my lap. "I thought you're in for an adventure, little one a very big adventure."

Chapter Twenty-Nine
Blown Up

Looking up at the beautiful house, just as the sun was setting, I felt for the first time in years, calm and very, very lucky. This was the start of a new and bright chapter in my life, and I really hoped that it would run smoother than my past. We had travelled across Europe by car me, Joy and Bonny. Taking it in turns to drive.

We of course had to show proof that we had been vaccinated but as this wasn't a holiday we didn't have to self-isolate. I was in my own property, after all.

It took us just four days to drive, to reach our destination. It was late and we were both exhausted. Opening the front door to my new home I tried the light switch, expecting to see light. Nothing, that's strange I thought, I had paid for the transfer of the electricity supply into my name following the sale, yet nothing was working. Fuck I thought great stuff, but my tired brain didn't want to deal with this till the morning. I heard Joy coming up the patio loaded with bags, Bonny trotting behind her. Dee what's wrong she asked. No electricity I replied, sounding very peed off, we will have to sort it out in the morning. I am gasping for a cuppa she said, do we have a small gas burner you know the one you take camping with you?

Somewhere in the back of the car, ok she said going to get it. I'm running the bath. I called out to her. I could hear her humming as she came through the door gas canister in her hand. I had just finished running the bath and stepped out to see what she was doing when Bang!!!

The kitchen was brightly lit and very hot, I didn't really understand what was going on till I heard Joy screaming, holding onto her arm, the door still wide open. What's wrong I cried, my arm, she screamed. I ran towards her panic rising smelling smoke everywhere the tea lights she had put in the kitchen to see, still smouldering and melting. The gas canister was rolling around on the patio, the flames dying out. As I ran to her, I could see the nasty blisters already starting to appear on her skin. Where is the dog, we couldn't see Bonny anywhere. We need to get you to the hospital, I said, grabbing a wet towel and wrapping it around her arm. Grabbing the car keys, I helped her get into the car and frantically started the engine. I was so tired I needed to take it easy driving before we had another accident. Driving as fast as I could I made my way back down the mountain, I didn't realise I was sobbing till I blinked at the road ahead. There was poor Bonny curled up shaking. I screeched to a halt, got out, grabbed her and put her on the back seat. The poor little girl looked petrified, but thankfully unharmed.

When we arrived at Kalamata Royal Hospital, the staff took one look at us and rushed us into a private room. We have a doggy, and we can't leave her in the car I said by this time I was crying. Sorry no Dogs allowed the Doctor replied, he looked kind and shocked by our appearance. I will look after her an elderly lady who was waiting to be seen said. Bring her here to me and I will wait outside with her for you. After I had thanked her, I went back inside, Joy was in a private side room, and I could hear her scream. I went in and saw her having her legs, arm and chin doused in red liquid, realising it was betadine the smell was horrific and every time they poured the betadine onto her burns, she screamed blue murder. Have you given her more medication. I cried, to the Doctor treating her, she is in agony. The kind Doctor took me to one side and said we have given her a lot of morphine we can't give her anymore. Please be patient. I sat next to Joy holding her hand while the nurses and doctors applied cream and used a razor to scrape the blisters that were forming in horrible lumps on her legs and arms. It was horrific the razors as it removed the swollen blisters, the sound was awful, they applied more antiseptic cream, more cold cream, and continued scraping, this went on for hours. Finally around 6 am we were told that we could go home, Joy was so bandaged up she looked like a mummy, I also had bandages to both my lower legs, I was in so much shock and reacting on autopilot that I didn't realise I was also burnt. Driving back home dawn was breaking, it was already warm. Looking at the gas gauge I realised I needed to fill up otherwise we would be stranded.

Joy was asleep and Bonny was curled up next to her. Driving back up the mountain I couldn't believe what had happened what a bloody start to a new life this was turning out to be I thought.

Chapter Thirty
The Village

When we got back to the village of Pedino, I noticed a few villagers walking toward the front porch of the house, gifts cakes and bags of drinks in their arms. I didn't understand what was going on. As we got out an old gentleman came towards me. He introduced himself, Gia Sou he said in Greek, my name is Socrates, I live further down in the village, he said pointing to his olive grove and Mani tower. We heard what has happened, please accept our help, anything you need we here for you, he spoke in broken English. I looked around at the people smiling, holding out their gifts to us, tokens of support and kindness.

They stayed till the early afternoon while Joy and I rested. Socrates and the villagers had somehow managed to get together tables, chairs and umbrellas, and had prepared a feast for us. We couldn't believe our tired eyes. There was food and drink everywhere.

They treated us like queens, nothing was to much for them, we ate the glorious food they had prepared for us, chatting to them explaining how the gas canister had exploded, they couldn't believe our bad luck. It was past midnight when they eventually left, hugging us and wishing us luck promising to help in any way they could. Such kindness and humanity, I was overwhelmed and so grateful to them. Exhausted from everything that had happened, wishing the neighbours a good night and thanking them for their kindness I went to bed and for the first time in years slept like a log.

Chapter Thirty-One
Animal Sanctuary

I woke up to the familiar sound of birds singing and the waves crashing on the nearby rocks. There was a soft breeze coming through the open window. I looked at the clock on my bedside table, five thirty a.m. yet I was wide awake, sweat already pouring off me. It was going to be another scorcher, for the past month since we had arrived the weather had been ridiculously hot, with temperatures reaching 43 degrees Celsius, it was such a difference to the grey cold weather of England, it was glorious. I was sitting on the vast balcony staring into the distance the blue green hues of the Mediterranean sea shone like precious gems. I sat lost in thought listening to the world as it slowly began to wake up. Crickets were chirping and birds were flying about their business. The soft waves in the distance could be heard going in and out of the shore, I watched as the fishermen in the distance gathered their wide nets full of fish shouting to each other laughing, the sun beating down on them a new day just beginning. I was so hot I decided to grab an ice cream from the freezer. Passing the big oak table, I noticed yesterday's newspaper. Taking it with me, I went back to my chair and started flicking through it, not really paying much attention to it. When an advert caught my attention, mainly because it was in English rather than Greek.

I read it carefully, my excitement growing... Animal Sanctuary for Sale—Applicants must have a genuine Love of Animals, please contact Andrea on 0030 2721555765. I heard Joy coming down the hallway and called her over showing her the advert, my face beaming. This was something I had always wanted to do, I wanted to make a difference to the poor creatures that needed help, and the number of strays in Greece broke my heart. I dear say if I hadn't trained to be a nurse, I would have chosen Veterinary Nursing instead. I loved animals just like Joy did and have always hated cruelty. I still had a fair amount of money left in my savings, and this opportunity was too good to miss. I really wanted to give it a go. "What do you think?" I asked Joy as she came towards me looking tired, the bandages from her burns had been removed, but her skin was still red and sore. She had spent most of the night working on her new novel, which was going well, and had been seen by a Literary Agent who wanted to publish it, I was pleased for her, she needed some good luck and a break, from the horror she had experienced on the streets. I thrust the advert in her face, nearly jumping up and down in my excitement, already envisioning the animals I was going to save and re home. I could see her reading it, a small smile forming on her lips. "I think your dream may have just come true; she knew how much I loved animals, ring her up to see what she says." I didn't need further encouragement and grabbing my mobile rang the number.

Summer is now in full swing in the village of Pedino, the few tourists can be seen enjoying its beautiful views and blue Green Mediterranean Sea, the new influx of visitors brings a new sense of hope to everyone and the possibility that things are perhaps getting better. Sometimes when the waves are crashing on the rocks, and the birds are singing I find it hard to remember what my life was like, I think back and remember how I used to rush around like a lunatic, working 14-hour shifts, worrying about deadlines and staff shortages. Above all, nearly losing my life to Covid, that memory never leaves my thoughts, and I do occasionally have nightmares where I am gasping for breath but there is no air and I am suffocating, because of my close brush with the Grim Reaper I try and make the most of each new day. Though the world is slowly recovering from the epidemic, things are very different here.

Greece has seen a decline in tourism because of the Covid lockdown which is very sad. Many have lost their homes and livelihoods, pretty much like they have in the UK. I hope when full sanctions are lifted that Greece will start recouping their loss off tourism. I have been extremely lucky, I sometimes pinch myself to see if the life I am leading now is real, and even though running the sanctuary has been hard work, as well as a battle of wills dealing with the Greek authorities, I am slowly but surely getting there, and looking at the donkeys, dogs and cats that my sanctuary has rescued and rehomed I feel very blessed. I eventually managed to train as a veterinary nurse, so I can now offer my nursing services to the poor strays. My heart breaks with the cruelty I see but at least I am able to help save a few animals, and those I haven't managed to re home, I have kept. Also, because the Peloponnese has quite a large expat residency, I have had a lot of help to re-home many of them. Joy eventually went back to the UK and studied journalism, she was hell bent on exposing the truth, and is now happily working in the job she loves. She has also informed me that she has just signed a literary publishing deal that's hopefully going to make her super rich. I'll keep my fingers crossed for her she could do with some good luck.

I am finally recovering from long Covid. I still get terrible brain fog, and need inhalers for my asthma, there are days when I feel so exhausted that I can hardly move, but the animals need me, so I push myself, to carry on, the glorious heat during the summer has done wonders for my arthritic bones. Life is simple but good. The strays and animals I have rescued are thriving and slowly but surely finding loving forever homes. Looking back at everything that has happened over the past decade I would have never envisioned my life ending like it has. Who would have ever thought that day when I'd had enough, and was willing to risk two grand, my career and the love of my life on a hunch that it would end this way. Because after all that's what it was, call it sixth sense, call it luck, call it what you want. It was a gamble, a huge one, one that would have made my mother turn in her grave. But it has miraculously worked out. I am a firm believer that sometimes the choices we make in life can literally change the course of our lives forever and sometimes just sometimes good things do happen to those who have a little hope. I do miss the NHS, I miss my patients, and my dear friend Phoebe, she is always in my thoughts, I am devastated that she is no longer here, so much more could have been done to help her. I hope to God that whatever government comes into power in the next elections, strive to make the NHS brilliant once again it deserves some TLC, hell it deserves a medal for carrying on and doing the best it can in the most horrible of situations and staff shortages. My life now is a far cry from the life I was used to. I sometimes wake up and think it's all a dream. I am eternally grateful to the wonderful Doctors and Nurses who saved my life, without them none of this would have been possible they are my heroes. I am very proud that I served as a nurse, and my patients and colleagues will stay in my heart and thoughts forever…